THE SACRED LITERATURE SERIES

THE PATH OF COMPASSION

The Sacred Literature Series of
the International Sacred Literature Trust

Titles in the series

Further titles in preparation

THE CHINESE BRAHMA'S NET SUTRA

The Path of Compassion

THE BODHISATTVA PRECEPTS

INTRODUCED AND TRANSLATED BY MARTINE BATCHELOR

*Foreword by
the Dalai Lama*

Published in cooperation with the
International Sacred Literature Trust

ALTAMIRA
PRESS

A Division of
ROWMAN & LITTLEFIELD PUBLISHERS, INC.
Walnut Creek • Lanham • New York • Oxford

For more information about the International Sacred Literature Trust,
please write to the ISLT at:
1st and 2nd Floors, 341 Lower Addiscombe Road
Croydon CR0 6RG, United Kingdom

ALTAMIRA PRESS
A division of Rowman & Littlefield Publishers, Inc.
1630 North Main Street, #367
Walnut Creek, CA 94596
www.altamirapress.com

Rowman & Littlefield Publishers, Inc.
A wholly owned subsidiary of The Rowman & Littlefield Publishing Group, Inc.
4501 Forbes Boulevard, Suite 200
Lanham, MD 20706

PO Box 317
Oxford
OX2 9RU, UK

Photoset in Sabon by Nothern Phototypesetting Co. Ltd., Bolton UK
Translation, Introduction and editorial matter copyright © 2004 by Martine Batchelor
Translation of the Tibetan Bodhisattva Vows in the Appendix is
copyright © FPMT Education Services

Library of Congress Cataloging-in-Publication Data

Batchelor, Martine.
The path of compassion / The Bodhisattva precepts ; introduced and translated
by Martine Batchelor ; foreword by the Dalai Lama.
p. cm. — (The sacred literature series)
Includes bibliographical references
ISBN 0-7591-0516-2 (hardcover : alk. paper)
ISBN 0-7591-0517-0 (pbk. : alk. paper)
I. Bodhisattvas. 2. Bodhisattva stages (Mahayana Buddhism) 3. Buddha (The
concept) I. Batchelor, Martine. II. Title. III. Series.
BX7795.E6A3 2004
289.6'092—dc22
2004011188

Printed in the United States of America

The International Sacred Literature Trust was established to promote understanding and open discussion between and within faiths and to give voice in today's world to the wisdom that speaks across time and traditions.

What resources do the sacred traditions of the world possess to respond to the great global threats of poverty, war, ecological disaster and spiritual despair?

Our starting-point is the sacred texts with their vision of a higher truth and their deep insights into the nature of humanity and the universe we inhabit. The publishing program is planned so that each faith community articulates its own teachings with the intention of enhancing its self-understanding as well as the understanding of those of other faiths and those of no faith.

The Trust especially encourages faiths to make available texts which are needed in translation for their own communities and also texts which are little known outside a particular tradition but which have the power to inspire, console, enlighten, and transform. These sources from the past become resources for the present and future when we make inspired use of them to guide us in shaping the contemporary world.

Our religious traditions are diverse but, as with the natural environment, we are discovering the global interdependence of human hearts and minds. The Trust invites all to participate in the modern experience of interfaith encounter and exchange which marks a new phase in the quest to discover our full humanity.

Contents

Foreword by His Holiness the Dalai Lama

A bodhisattva is one who, out of love and compassion, has attained a realization of *bodhichitta*, which is a mental state characterized by a spontaneous and genuine aspiration to attain full enlightenment in order to be of benefit to all living beings. Indeed, the foundation of all Mahayana Buddhist doctrine is this very altruistic thought of *bodhichitta*, which in turn depends on the practice of kindness and compassion.

When a bodhisattva actually engages in training, he or she not only meditates on qualities like compassion and altruism, but actually engages in conduct such as giving and ethical discipline that are related to the direct benefit of sentient beings. So meditation and practical application mutually complement each other, which is why a bodhisattva can be recognized by his or her conduct as described in the following verse:

> Just the presence of the ocean is understood by the gulls above it
> And the presence of fire by smoke,
> Similarly, one who holds the lineage of a wise bodhisattva can be recognized
> By observing his external behaviour.

The Buddha gave clear instructions about how a bodhisattva should preserve and nurture the altruistic aspiration to enlightenment that are contained in the scriptures of the various Mahayana traditions. The Bodhisattva Precepts as found in the *Brahma's Net Sutra* of the Chinese and Korean traditions have laid the foundation of an ethical way of life and the essential ground to a life of compassion for many Buddhists in East Asia since ancient times. We live in an era in which I believe it is extremely important to foster harmony and respect among all religious traditions. Therefore, I believe it is significant that such a seminal text be made more widely available in an English translation and I congratulate the translator, the International Sacred Literature Trust and AltaMira Press for making this book, *The Path of Compassion*, available Readers, whether or not they are Buddhist, will find that these precepts encourage us, in a very practical way, to protect life in all its forms and work towards a more peaceful and understanding world; goals that we all can admire.

1 September 2003

Acknowledgements

I would like to thank Robert Buswell Jr, Merry Colony, Philippe Cornu, the Revd Issho Fujita, Peter Gregory, Hyung-hi Jong, Mr and Mrs Kim, Young In Ko, Josh Krieger, Song Gon Lee, Hyung-hi May, Jacques May, Ven. Constance Miller, Andrew Olendzki, Renée Rousso, Jeremy Russell, Gregory Schopen, Jeff Shore, Ally Stott and Jong-Kweon Yi for their invaluable help. I am grateful to the Foundation for the Preservation of the Mahayana Tradition (FPMT) for permission to reprint their translation of the Tibetan Bodhisattva vows, and to the librarians of the Hautes Etudes Chinoises at the Collège de France, Paris, for their kindness. I am indebted to Malcolm Gerratt and Paulène Fallows for their skilful editing. I am deeply grateful to my husband, Stephen Batchelor, for his unstinting support, kindness and understanding.

Introduction

A living tradition

In May 1975, I arrived in the Korean monastery of Songgwang, nestled deep in the mountains. I crossed an ancient bridge and met a bustling crowd. There were several hundred people, monks and nuns and lay followers, men and women, attending the commemoration of the death of the founder of the temple, Master Bojo Bulil, also known as Chinul (1158–1210). This commemoration lasted three days. Its essential components were the receiving of the bodhisattva precepts and, beforehand, hearing discourses and explanations given by learned teachers on the *Brahma's Net Sutra*. It was an opportunity for people to receive the bodhisattva precepts for the first time and in performing that act to enter the Buddhist creed formally. They were given a Buddhist name and a certificate inscribed with the list of the ten major and forty-eight secondary bodhisattva precepts as found in the *Brahma's Net Sutra*.

A high point of the ceremony was the symbolic burning of the arm that all feared and were uplifted by at the same time. Hundreds of people would be gathered in the main Buddha hall, all kneeling with their left arms bared. Monks and nuns would pass among them and stick a tiny piece of wick on the inside of each person's forearm; at a given signal they would light it and then allow it to extinguish itself on the skin. This was a symbol of both renunciation and purity. Just before anyone received the pure

1

bodhisattva precepts, their defilements were symbolically burnt to demonstrate their commitment to a pure, ethical and compassionate life. At the end of the ceremony, all would gather in the large courtyard. After placing their certificate in a white envelope, which they tied to their heads with a scarf or a string, they would chant while walking in single file along a special route that represented the interdependence and interconnection of all things.

Different Buddhist traditions will express and practise compassion in diverse ways. In the Indian Mahayana tradition that greatly influenced Tibetan Buddhism, Shantideva (eighth century CE) explained in *A Guide to the Bodhisattva's Way of Life* the practice of the exchange of self for others. He encouraged practitioners to consider various situations from the point of view and experience of others:

> Thus sentient beings should be my main (concern).
> Whatever I behold upon my body
> I should rob and use
> For the benefit of others.

Similar sentiments are expressed throughout the *Brahma's Net Sutra*. In the Theravada traditions of Thailand, Sri Lanka and Burma we find the meditative practice of loving-kindness and compassion. In the Zen traditions of China, Korea or Japan, there is the essential vow of saving all sentient beings and the cultivation of the bodhisattva precepts that are laid out in the *Brahma's Net Sutra*.

After my arrival at the monastery of Songgwang, I decided to become a Buddhist nun. It was while living as a Zen nun in this monastery that I became interested in the *Brahma's Net Sutra*, of which we listened to a recitation at least once a month. As my understanding of Korean improved I realized that this text was the source of the compassionate attitude that I found in the monastery, and it influenced strongly the way in which my teacher, Master Kusan, would behave. Whenever Master Kusan met an animal, he would pat it on the head, if he could, and say a few quiet words. One day I dared to ask him what he was saying. He replied that he was wishing for the animal to give rise to the mind of awakening in a future life. This is part of the forty-fifth secondary precept, in which a disciple of the Buddha is strongly encouraged to be compassionate in mind whenever he encounters any living being and to wish it to be liberated from suffering.

In Korea each year many laypeople receive the bodhisattva precepts anew. The monks and the nuns, as I mentioned above, do so every month. They are not seen as rules and regulations that must be accepted once and adhered to for all time; they are treasured as the foundation for an attitude of compassion to all of life. At the same time it is acknowledged that one is only human, prone to making mistakes and reverting to self-centredness, so one needs to be reminded again and again of one of the essential components of the Buddhist path: compassion.

The *Brahma's Net Sutra* has been the basic ethical text for Chinese, Korean and Japanese Buddhists for the last fifteen hundred years. Ethics can be applied and followed for different reasons: to conform to society's standards, for fear of future punishment, out of guilt for original sin or from compassion for life, and to help life develop and grow. This text shows us that the foundation of an ethical life is compassion and awareness. The need for compassion is set out very clearly – it is referred to in more than twenty-two of the fifty-eight precepts – while awareness is implied in the way the various precepts are formulated. Their aim is to make us reflect on our behaviour and how it can have a negative and painful impact on us and on others.

The Buddha: the first bodhisattva

The bodhisattva precepts are the ethical path that a disciple of the Buddha endeavours to follow so as to fulfil his or her potential as a human being who shares this world with others and is both aware of and responsive to their pains. The duty of a bodhisattva is often mentioned in the *Brahma's Net Sutra* as that of being compassionate and leading others to liberation and awakening.

Two and a half thousand years ago, Siddhartha Gautama, the future Shakyamuni Buddha, left his home in Kapilavastu (India) to discover how to end suffering. In his time there were different teachers living a life of practice and mendicancy with their disciples. After practising with some of them, Siddhartha Gautama decided to find a practice that would truly end suffering and not just lead to high meditative states of consciousness. He spent seven years as a wandering mendicant then sat under the bodhi tree. Six days later he reached full awakening to the causes of suffering – grasping and self-centredness – and to the way leading to its end: the middle path between asceticism and self-indulgence. This middle way required the Buddha's followers to cultivate the eightfold path of authentic vision, motive, speech, action, livelihood, effort, mindfulness and concentration.

The term *bodhisattva* can be interpreted as follows. Bodhi means "awakening". In Buddhism three different types of awakening are referred to: the awakening of the hearer (*sravaka*) or noble disciple, that of a Buddha who practises and awakens on his own (*pratyeka-buddha*), and the perfect and complete awakening of a Buddha who turns the wheel of Dharma. *Sattva* in general means "living being". So a bodhisattva is a being dedicated to awakening.[1]

The term at first referred only to the historical Buddha, Shakyamuni, before his awakening and in his earlier lives as known in the *Jataka* tales. These described his path of practice through many lives to purify himself and to perfect many different qualities, such as altruism, so that in his last life he could become the fully awakened Buddha. One well-known *Jataka* tale tells of the Buddha in a previous life throwing himself off a cliff so that on his death a starving tigress could feed herself and give milk to her cubs. Many of the stories describe great sacrifice but also great compassion and wisdom. This notion of the Buddha as bodhisattva implied that there was only one bodhisattva at a time working through many aeons to become a Buddha. Then in the presence of that Buddha the next bodhisattva would take the vow to become the next Buddha. In our aeon and in our world the next Buddha will be Maitreya.

Later the term *bodhisattva* broadened to include anyone special who had the qualities to become a Buddha or who was to become a Buddha. It then expanded further to denote sincere practitioners who dedicated themselves to the welfare of others while cultivating the Perfections (*paramitas*), the six or ten qualities enabling one to reach the shore of awakening. There are two series of these. The first consists of generosity, ethics, renunciation, wisdom, effort, patience, determination towards truth, resolve, loving-kindness and equanimity; the second consists of generosity, ethics, patience, effort, meditation and wisdom, as well as skill in means, making vows, strength of purpose and knowledge.

Eventually the epithet *bodhisattva* came to be applied to anyone who aspired to awaken for the sake of all. In this context one became a bodhisattva upon making the vow to dedicate oneself to awakening for the sake of all beings. In the Korean Zen tradition this resolution is contained in the four vows that are recited at any important ceremony:

> Sentient beings are numberless, I vow to save them all,
> Defilements are inexhaustible, I vow to cut them off,
> Dharma gates are limitless, I vow to learn them all,
> The Buddha's way is unsurpassable, I vow to accomplish it.

A distinction was made between the earthly and the transcendent bodhisattvas. The earthly bodhisattvas are those who show a high degree of compassion and altruism and a deep resolve to attain awakening. The transcendent bodhisattvas have fully developed all the Perfections and realized Buddhahood but are continually reborn to help beings in need. They represent various qualities, for instance compassion, wisdom or fine deeds. One well-known example is the Bodhisattva Avalokitesvara, the bodhisattva of compassion. He/she is represented with a thousand eyes and hands so that he/she can see the suffering and hear the cry of the world and respond to it compassionately. In modern times His Holiness the fourteenth Dalai Lama is regarded as an incarnation of the bodhisattva of compassion, Avalokitesvara. Two of his main teachings are kindness and compassion.

Mahayana: the Great Vehicle

The word Buddha means "awakened", in two senses: the one who awakened himself and the one who awakened others. These two definitions represent the two great currents in Buddhism, the Hinayana and the Mahayana. The Hinayana suggests the Buddha as the ideal for those who want to awaken themselves. The Mahayana presents the Buddha as an example to those who strive for the liberation of others. In the Great Vehicle the emphasis is on the active cultivation of certain virtues, such as generosity, patience and ethics, but especially benevolence and compassion. The ideal of the accomplished one, the *arhat*, in the Hinaya school was restraint, renunciation and practice in order to cut more effectively the links to the endless round of rebirth. The ideal of the realized being in the Great Vehicle is awakening for the sake of all beings. The Mahayana is characterized by an affirmation of the world and of life, lofty religious ideals, a complex cosmology and mythology, and new or radically developed philosophical positions, all of which are apparent in the *Brahma's Net Sutra*.

In the bodhisattva precepts, there are many references to the word Mahayana. Mahayana literally means "great vehicle" and Hinayana "small vehicle". Some precepts refer directly to studying, sustaining and propagating the Mahayana tradition. In the sixth major precept, for example, the bodhisattva is encouraged to help misguided beings to give rise to faith in the Mahayana and in the thirty-ninth to expound the sutras of the Mahayana for the sake of sentient beings. The eighth secondary precept requires the Buddha's disciple not to go intentionally against the Mahayana. In the sixteenth, thirty-fifth and forty-fourth secondary precepts it is suggested that a bodhisattva should learn, study and recite the sutras of the Mahayana. In the twenty-fourth secondary precept it is an offence deliberately to study the *Abhidharma* commentaries of the Hinayana instead of the sutras of the Mahayana. According to the thirty-fourth secondary precept, "One must always maintain faith in the Mahayana . . . [and] not give rise even for a moment to the attitude of the Hinayana."

These forceful statements about the Mahayana show that the *Brahma's Net Sutra* is a Mahayanist text and that the precepts are used to defend and argue the case for the Mahayana. One of the challenges that confront us when working with some religious texts is that, however profound they are, they are intended partly to defend and promote the superiority of their tradition against any other. Here there is one main opponent, the Hinayana. No school will refer to itself as Hinayana or "small vehicle"; that is a term invented by the Mahayanists. They are the ones with the greater tradition, the other Buddhist schools have the lesser ones. The Mahayanists will give good reasons for their name: they are more universal, their scope is wider and they have more practices than earlier schools. It seems that any position works better if there is *opp*osition. It would be interesting to see whether a school of thought or religion could arise without defining itself as being in opposition to any other school.

In this regard one could view the present text as falling short of its universalist and all-compassionate message. When I started to translate those passages that seemed to be critical of the Hinayana and the outsiders, I was quite concerned, but a learned monk whom I asked about it told me not to take this too seriously and that it was part of a way of defining oneself in ancient times. Since then, in reading different sacred texts I have often noticed the insertion of polemical passages that refer to debates and discussions that took place at particular times in history. Personally I prefer not to use the term Hinayana, but in discussing the Mahayana I have to do so. As I use the term here I do not mean it to be derogatory, but simply to designate those early Buddhist schools to which the Mahayana tradition that reached China felt opposed and against which it defined itself. In defining a tradition in contradistinction to one's own, it is all too easy to misrepresent the former to the extent of caricaturing it, and I am anxious to avoid this.

There is no unanimity among Western scholars about exactly how, when or where the Mahayana came into being. The use of *maha* ("great") to qualify a Buddhist school appeared in the fourth century BCE, the time of the first schism in the Buddhist community. At what became known as the Council of Vesali two factions arose: a liberal one and a more conservative one. The liberal group called itself the Mahasanghika (the great community); the other group was known as the Sthaviras (the elders). Over the centuries there was further dissension and fragmentation among the Sthaviras. The most important breakaway group was known as the Sarvastivada (literally, the teaching that everything exists).

The term *Hinayana* was initially applied to all the early schools of Buddhism. In the beginning Mahayana and Hinayana coexisted in India and then started to spread in various directions. Eventually the Mahayana traditions began to dominate in East and Central Asia. Hinayana schools spread more slowly and later this term referred to the only remaining Hinayana school, which called itself Theravada (the teaching of the elders). This school developed in Sri Lanka and spread to South-East Asia; it exists to this day in Sri Lanka, Thailand and Burma.

A universal doctrine

The Mahayana appeared in its more elaborate form in the second century CE . A reform movement as well as the natural development of pre-Mahayana Buddhism, it is considered to be a continuation of earlier Buddhist doctrine and practices formulated and expanded by creative thinkers and practitioners. One of the main expanded doctrines was that of the bodhisattva ideal. Another important theoretical development was the doctrine of emptiness. The idea of emptiness is an intensification of the doctrine of no-self taught by the Buddha. One is told in the thirtieth secondary precept not to proclaim that things are empty when showing a grasping at existence. In the concept of emptiness there are two main points: the fact that nothing exists on its own and independently, and the practice of non-grasping. Non-grasping follows from the fact that nothing is imbued with an inherent substance and therefore there is nothing to grasp. Everything is conditional and depends upon circumstances and conditions for its arising and ceasing. Non-grasping also brings peace, since everything is impermanent and changing; suffering will ensue when things that are unreliable are grasped.

It is thought by some scholars that one of the conditions whereby the Mahayana evolved was the desire by the lay disciples of the Buddha's teaching to be more involved in the religion and the practice. This made the aim of the religion loftier and more relevant to them at the same time. It may have made possible a significant move towards a less ascetic and monastic religion in which laypeople could have a more prominent and participatory role. The Great Vehicle is more universalist than other Buddhist schools in that its stated aim is for all to attain Buddhahood, not just a select holy few. So the path starts with the aspiration to awakening which is spoken in a vow and then articulated in a series of stages that I will look at in detail below.

One feature of the special vows of the bodhisattva is the resolve to delay his or her own nirvana until all beings have become liberated. A further element is the idea of transmitting to other beings the merits generated by one's practice of meditation and the cultivation of various Buddhist virtues. The vow of the bodhisattva was the ground for the development of religious practices in which the dedication of merits became part of the bodhisattva ideal. There is some evidence in inscriptions on ancient sculptures in India that the belief in the transference of merit was playing an important part in the religious Buddhist life even before the rise of the Mahayana. Buddhists believed that good thoughts and actions generated merits that would help towards a better rebirth. Early Buddhists thought that the effects of the merits could apply only to themselves. Over time in both the Hinayana and the Mahayana the idea developed that merits could be shared or transferred and, by implication, that they could also help one to attain liberation. When the two ideas were combined it became possible for a person to offer his or her merit for the liberation of relatives who had died.

Another development in the Mahayana was that of its cosmology and mythology. In the early discourses, the Buddha describes six realms of existence (celestial gods, titans, humans, animals, hungry ghosts and hellish realms) in which beings are born through the force of karma. They were trying to represent the working of moral cause and effect (also known as karma) over many lives. Reincarnation was already a belief and part of the cultural and religious environment in the India of two and a half thousand years ago. This cosmology was used in Buddhist texts to encourage Buddhist ethics and meritorious actions. In early Buddhist cosmology there were already descriptions of other worlds coexisting with this one. The Mahayanists expanded this notion further into an astonishing plurality of worlds and within each the existence of a Buddha as is described in the introduction to the *Brahma's Net Sutra*, where a Shakyamuni Buddha appears in each of the hundred million worlds that are mentioned.

In both Hinayana and Mahayana there was also the elaboration of the former lives of the historical Buddha Shakyamuni and the intensifying cultivation of devotion to former Buddhas. Shakyamuni Buddha saw himself as one in a series of awakened beings, the seventh to have appeared in the course of the current aeon. (A main list of seven previous Buddhas is mentioned in the *Brahma's Net Sutra* in the twenty-eighth and forty-second secondary precepts.) In Mahayana Buddhism numerous Buddhas are recognized as existing in different worlds at all times. This emphasizes the fact that Shakyamuni Buddha is the Buddha for his age and that his teaching can respond to the needs of the people in his times.

One of the early Buddhas adopted by the Mahayana as a symbol of ultimate reality is Vairocana Buddha ("the luminous one"). He is seen as representing Buddhism's profound doctrines on emptiness and the interpenetration of all things. As C. D. Orzech explains: "Vairocana represents ultimate reality and at the same time permeates all levels of the manifest cosmos and the beings in it. The universe is his infinite body. All things are in him, and his presence shines in all things."[2]

It is stated in the introduction to the *Brahma's Net Sutra* that the bodhisattva precepts themselves arose out of the fundamental Dharma words of Rocana Buddha, who is seen as the original being of the Buddha in the text. Vairocana and Rocana are sometimes considered to be the same, sometimes different. In the *Avatamsaka Sutra*, a seminal text for Mahayana Buddhism that was translated into Chinese by Buddhabhadra in 418–20, shortly before the *Brahma's Net Sutra* was written, a slight distinction seems to be made between the two: Vairocana is designated as the "fundamental body" of the Buddha and Rocana as the "enjoyment body". This classification comes from the Mahayanist doctrines of the three bodies of the Buddha, regarded as three aspects of the awakening of the Buddha. The Buddha is endowed with the "enjoyment body" as a result of his previous virtuous actions and his accumulated merits. This "enjoyment body", which represents the Buddha as an object of devotion, is sometimes translated as "communal enjoyment" as it is considered to be enjoyment for others.

After Buddhism entered Japan in the sixth century, the *Brahma's Net Sutra* remained very influential for some centuries. The passage in the introduction about Rocana Buddha and the hundred million worlds so impressed Emperor Shomu in 744 CE that he was inspired to build a great Buddha sculpture in Nara, the Daibutsu. It was to be a representation of Rocana Buddha and the assembly of Buddhas as described in the *Brahma's Net Sutra*. On each of the sculpted lotus flowers on which this immense Buddha rested, every one of the thousand great Shakyamunis and their worlds was represented.

The emergence of the Mahayana was also the decisive factor for great literary creative energy, and many different Mahayanist groups started to produce sutras following the edict of King Asoka (third century BCE), who proclaimed: "Whatever is well spoken is the word of the Buddha." One of the messages of these sutras was that the Buddha-nature belongs to all beings without exception, even if they are unaware of it. This in turn makes possible the equality of all beings that will engender great compassion, which will be directed equally towards all beings.

This equality is a prominent feature of the message of the bodhisattva precepts. In "The Origin of the Bodhisattva Precepts" it is clearly stated that "all sentient beings are endowed with the Buddha-nature. And . . . the basic cause [i.e. the Buddha-nature] is always present [in beings]." In this text we find long lists of different types of being. The first such list appears in the introduction and is quite exhaustive: "kings, princes, government officials, ministers of state, bhikshus, bhikshunis, celestials of the eighteen realms of Brahma, lords of the six realms of desire, ordinary people, eunuchs, sensuous men or women, servants, one of the eight kinds of demons, guardian spirits, animals, spirits". In the fortieth secondary precept hermaphrodites and ghosts are added to the list. The author seemed to be trying to include as many forms of being as possible and not to forget any.

Stages on the path

In the life of the bodhisattva there are two essential moments: when he or she first gives rise to the mind of awakening by pledging himself or herself to attain supreme awakening for the benefit of all beings and when he or she realizes the supreme and complete awakening that makes him or her a Buddha. A long gap can exist between these two moments. After cultivating the Perfections for many lifetimes as the Buddha did, and thus accumulating merits, a bodhisattva must develop and pass through various stages to attain Buddhahood.

At the beginning in India certain texts declared that there were four stages on the bodhisattva path. Later texts suggested a bodhisattva development in seven stages. Finally, a course in ten stages was accepted by most Buddhist schools. Even with this division into ten stages, however, there is not complete agreement on the name and description of each stage. Different texts give different classifications.

The *Brahma's Net Sutra* has its own unique classification that describes forty stages of development on the bodhisattva path in four sets of ten steps. Several times throughout the text these forty stages are referred to in different ways. In the introduction, the bodhisattvas of the ten Initial Stages, of the ten Developmental Stages, of the ten Diamond Stages and of the ten Grounds are mentioned. At the end of the ten major precepts it is stated that if one transgresses the precepts one will lose the position one has attained among these forty stages. In the fifteenth secondary precept, progress through the first thirty stages is referred to. In the thirty-fifth secondary precept, on "Making vows", one is encouraged to seek instruction on these forty stages. In the forty-first secondary precept the "developmental" nature is mentioned.

1. *The ten Initial Stages*
   renunciation
   ethics
   patience
   zeal
   mediiaiion
   wisdom
   resolve
   guarding the Dharma
   joy
   blessing (by the Buddha)

These initial stages are the qualities that a bodhisattva has to cultivate at the beginning. In order to be dedicated sincerely to the path, one needs to be less involved in material things of the world as well as fame and renown. The following five qualities are five of the ten Perfections. One needs to be ethical in one's relationship with others; to have patience in difficult situations; to practise diligently; to meditate in order to pacify and clarify the body, heart and mind; and to cultivate the wisdom of listening and reflecting. Then it is essential to have the resolve to continue on this path and to guard it carefully to allow it to blossom. In so doing one fosters great joy in being alive, being able to practise, and being of help to others. The bodhisattva rejoices at having entered on the path of awakening and compassion. One feels blessed by the Buddha when one's heart and mind open and it becomes easier to lead the life of a bodhisattva.

2. *The ten Developmental Stages*
   loving-kindness
   compassion
   joy
   renunciation
   giving alms

good discourse
altruism
mutuality
meditation
wisdom

These are the qualities one must cultivate in order to deepen one's practice when one aspires to become a bodhisattva. Loving-kindness and compassion towards others are essential components of the practice, for they allow us to benefit others but also to open and dissolve self-centredness. Joy is mentioned again, this time rejoicing in the happiness of others and in their good fortune. Not only does this show appreciation and awareness of others but it will increase one's own joy as well. Renunciation in the developmental stage means relinquishing one's hold on possessions in order to give generously to those who ask and are in need. After practising for a while one can be of help to others by sharing knowledge and experience of the Buddha's teachings and thus cultivating good discourse. At this stage altruism is generated and, by discovering mutuality, one feels connected and interdependent with the whole world. As the meditation deepens, one becomes calmer and clearer. Wisdom increases as one understands and experiences for oneself the impermanence, unreliability and conditionality of the world that one encounters.

3. *The ten Diamond Stages*
    faith
    remembrance
    transference of one's own merits to others
    understanding
    uprightness
    no-retreat
    Mahayana
    formlessness
    wisdom
    indestructibility

14

As one perseveres on the bodhisattva path, faith in one's potential to become a Buddha strengthens, and the virtues of the path and of the teachings are remembered constantly. Any merit one might have accumulated through skilful or kind actions is willingly transferred to others. The bodhisattva also penetrates and understands deeply the truths shown by the Buddha. He or she is straight and upright in his or her dealings with the world and in the practice. From now on one can no longer regress on the bodhisattva path; one's faith, determination and experiences are too deep and part of one's very being. The practice is firmly based on the Mahayana ideals and their foundation of universality. When one at last becomes aware of formlessness or emptiness one starts to perceive that things are not as fixed or as solid as they appear to be. They do not exist in and of themselves. As it is stated at the end of the *Brahma's Net Sutra*:

> All the true forms of all Dharmas
> are neither born nor do they perish.
> They never recur yet never cease.
> They are neither the same nor different.
> And likewise they neither come nor go.

A bodhisattva tries to live from that understanding. The ninth Diamond Stage is wisdom. First there was the wisdom of listening, then the wisdom of reflecting, and finally one gains the wisdom that comes from understanding and experiencing personally the truths of the Buddha's teachings. The last Diamond Stage is indestructibility. In Buddhism the diamond is a symbol of hardness, indestructibility and power. It represents the stage at which the bodhisattva has vanquished all delusions.

4. The ten Grounds
> equality
> fine wisdom
> light
> brilliant flame
> illuminating wisdom
> beautiful brightness

accomplishment
Buddha's roar
flower adornment
entrance into the Buddha's realm

These ten Grounds are the ones found in the *Brahma's Net Sutra*. They are also known as the ten sagely positions. The first thirty positions explain and present the cultivation and practices of the bodhisattva. The ten Grounds demonstrate what he or she has achieved. First the state of equality is attained, in which the bodhisattva adopts the same attitude towards all beings. He or she gives equally to all beings without distinction material things, the Dharma and confidence against fear. Secondly the bodhisattva attains fine discriminative wisdom, knowing the nature of all dharmas and when and how to save sentient beings. From the second ground to the sixth, wisdom is developed to brighter and brighter degrees. Thirdly the bodhisattva becomes like a radiant light and has the ability to know, explain and expound all the Buddha's teaching in a bright and clear manner. Fourthly the bodhisattva is like a bright flame. He or she makes no distinctions between the relative and the absolute. At that stage one realizes that the Buddha's world is the same as the mundane world.

In the fifth stage, that of illuminating wisdom, the bodhisattva knows fully the principles of causality, and his or her mastery of skilful means benefits many beings. In the sixth ground, of beautiful brightness, the bodhisattva manifests a variety of wisdoms that enables him or her to transform countless sentient beings. At the stage of fulfilment the bodhisattva has completely cultivated all the Perfections and attained all there is to attain in terms of wisdom, compassion and acquiring merits. Reaching the eighth ground, the Buddha's roar, the bodhisattva's spiritual knowledge is equivalent to that of the Buddha. He or she is a great teacher and guide who can succour beings in difficulties by virtue of his or her great compassion and wisdom. The bodhisattva's teaching is like the roaring of the lion. Reaching the flower adornment ground, the bodhisattva's activities are manifested and blossom like a flower to reach everyone. All beings are seen as being one's father or mother, and one is able to transform oneself skilfully so as to serve as many beings as possible. When the bodhisattva attains the tenth ground he or she penetrates the Buddha's realm and achieves liberation. Immaculate and free from all attachments, one is said to be (nearly) the equal of the Buddha.

Ethics

Some scholars see the distinction between the Hinayana and the Mahayana ethics as the difference between ethics founded on the concept of the Buddha-nature and those founded on the concept of personal cultivation. The idea of the intrinsic Buddha-nature gave the conviction that awakening led one to live in an authentically ethical manner. According to this, ethics is no longer a discipline but arises spontaneously out of inner compassion and wisdom. As is stated clearly in "The Origin of the Bodhisattva Precepts":

> Because all sentient beings are endowed with the Buddha-nature, they possess form, thought and consciousness. Thought and consciousness are thus contained within the ethical principle of the Buddha-nature. And because the basic cause [i.e. the Buddha-nature] is always present [in beings], the Dharma-body is likewise always there. As a result of these conditions, the ten major ethical precepts come into being.

There is therefore a strong connection between the existence of the Buddha-nature and the origin and cultivation of the precepts.

It follows that the precepts are essential to the path of liberation. Beautiful metaphors are used to describe their importance and value. To keep the precepts is like seeing the light of a fire in a dark place, like a poor man finding a jewel, like a sick person recovering his or her health, like a prisoner being released. It is also like returning home. The precepts are also compared to a brilliant lamp, a most precious mirror and valuable gems. There is the very strong idea that being ethical is like becoming a light; it is like becoming illuminated. Thus the precepts are seen not as a prison or a gag but as a liberating factor. In practical terms it means that we become brighter and clearer. If we look into our experience, if we are ethical in this compassionate and wise way, we do feel lighter and clearer and more at peace with ourselves, and with the world that surrounds us.

The Buddhist monastic rule (*vinaya*) is traditionally held to have been created by the Buddha over his lifetime. At the beginning there were no specific precepts. To become a monk or a nun it was necessary merely to pronounce a few words. As the community developed, however, and problematic incidents occurred that disturbed either the community of monastics or the lay followers, the Buddha started to lay down certain rules relating to each incident. Some of these precepts are anachronistic now because they responded to events that happened two and a half thousand years ago in a very different cultural context. For example, one of the precepts is that a monk must not speak the Dharma to someone who holds a parasol, because in India at that time only a person of high rank would have a parasol held over them. To listen to the Dharma without a parasol would be a sign of humility and openness.

After the death of the Buddha the precepts were classified in diverse categories of gravity, then collected, compiled, commented upon and given the name *vinaya*. This is the code of discipline that is included in the Buddhist Canon and summarized in the text known as *Pratimoksha*, which is read at the *uposatha* (purification) ceremony, as stated in the thirty-seventh secondary precept for the *Brahma's Net Sutra*. Traditionally this text is recited by the whole community of monastics every fifteen days, at the full moon and new moon, after the monastics have confessed the breaking of any of these precepts to another monk or nun.

The precepts have been seen by most schools of Buddhism as an essential ingredient of the path. In Buddhism there are considered to be three main forms of training: ethics, meditation and wisdom. Ethics is considered essential for different reasons. In terms of restraint, by keeping one's impulses and desires in check one will achieve liberation more easily, as there will be less grasping and fewer obstacles. There is also a social aspect to the precepts, as they contribute to greater harmony of the monastic community or in social interaction. Moreover, they increase the lay followers' respect for the monastics as the latter are dedicated to living a pure life, which in turn makes them worthy of the support and dona-tions of the lay community. In the early Hinayana schools, ethics was concerned for the well-being of the person and that in turn led to the well-being of others. As it was stated, "He who protects himself protects others; he who protects others protects himself."[3]

Mahayana ethics kept the basic elements found in the earlier tra-ditions but added to them and expanded their scope. As Frank E. Reynolds and Robert Campany explain: "The ethical ideal of the Mahayana combined the social virtues of a righteous householder with the ascetic ideals of a meditating monk, bridging what was perceived by its proponents as a gap between monastic and popu-lar Buddhism."[4] The Mahayanist monks continued to uphold the pre-Mahayana *Vinaya*. And in China this discipline was comple-mented by the discipline of the bodhisattva as found in the *Brahma's Net Sutra*.

There are different kinds of ordination for the monks, nuns and lay followers. For the lay followers there are first the five precepts present in all Buddhist traditions: not to kill, not to steal, not to have improper sexual intercourse, not to lie, not to drink alcohol. In the Theravada and the Tibetan tradition people can receive eight precepts. These are generally taken on *uposatha* day, when lay fol-lowers go to the temple. The eight precepts add the following three to the five above: no sitting on a high seat; no wearing of perfumes or participating in or attending performances of dance and music, and no eating after midday. The novice monks and nuns generally take ten precepts, and then thirty-six in the Tibetan tradition. The fully ordained monks might have 227, 250 or 253 precepts accord-ing to the *vinaya* they follow, and the nuns 311, 348 or 364 pre-cepts. In Korea the fully ordained monks (250 precepts) recite the *vinaya* together with the precept master on a certain appointed day. Alternatively, fifteen days later they are joined by the rest of the community (postulants, novices and lay followers) for the recitation of the *Brahma's Net Sutra*. Before the *Brahma's Net Sutra*, the lay followers and the monastics took different sets of precepts. Since the bodhisattva precepts are taken by both, this fits in with the universalist pattern of the Mahayana.

The most serious faults were called *parajikas* (literally "defeat") and entailed expulsion from the order in the Pali tradition. There are different types of grave faults according to the specific *vinaya*. In general there are four for the monks (sexual intercourse, stealing, killing, falsely claiming to be awakened) and eight for the nuns. Mahayana ethics were more flexible and could be altered in certain circumstances. In the Hinayana the intention and the action are seen as equally important, whereas in the Mahayana the intention is sometimes regarded as paramount. To commit a grave fault is not necessarily considered a *parajika* in the Mahayana if it is for the benefit of others. Thus there is a danger in the Mahayana of misinterpretation and becoming lax, and in the Hinayana tradition one runs the opposite risk of becoming legalistic and narrow. It is noticeable that in the *Brahma's Net Sutra* there is a distinction between what are considered extremely serious transgressions and what are seen as secondary defiling offences. In this way the bodhisattva *vinaya* follows the schema of the *vinaya* of the monastics.

The precepts in the Hinayana schools must be received in the presence of ten monks, three of whom will act as teachers. The bodhisattva precepts can be taken by oneself under certain conditions. As is explained in the twenty-third secondary precept, if one wishes to receive the bodhisattva precepts on one's own, one need only make a sincere vow before a Buddha image and repent. If this is followed by auspicious signs, then the precepts are considered as taken and received. This was regarded as a major departure from the discipline of the Hinayana, which was more formalistic. Here we are starting to see a do-it-yourself attitude that avoids relying on institutions and anticipates future changes to ethics in Buddhism that will culminate in the various modes of ethics found today in the East and the West.

Over time, slightly different versions of the *vinaya* appeared as various Buddhist schools developed. For example, there are the Theravada Vinaya with 227 precepts for monks and 311 for nuns, the Dharmagupta Vinaya (250 precepts for the monks and 348 for nuns), the Sarvastivada Vinaya, and so on. The Dharmagupta Vinaya became the *vinaya* for the monks and nuns in China. The complete text of the Vinaya of the Dharmagupta school was translated in 408 by Buddhayasas, the Vinaya of the Sarvastivadin by Kumarajiva in 404, and the Vinaya of the Mahasanghika in 416 by Buddhabhadra. There was also a translation of the Vinaya of the Mahisasaka made by Buddhajiva from Kashmir between 424 and 426. All this translation activity of different *vinaya* texts at the beginning of the fifth century in China must have favoured the creation of the *Brahma's Net Sutra* between 440 and 480.

Although Buddhism entered China in the first century CE, the order of monks and nuns did not become well established before the fourth century. At the beginning, because the *vinaya* texts had not been transmitted, there were no proper rules, but those created by eminent teachers worried about the proper conduct for the monastics like Tao-an (died c.385). The translation of the complete *vinaya* texts at the beginning of the fifth century and the active following of the precepts helped the establishment of a strong monastic community in China.

When the *Brahma's Net Sutra* came to Japan, the bodhisattva precepts were adopted by the Tendai monks in 822 as the standard discipline instead of the 250 precepts of the Dharmagupta Vinaya. Saicho (767–822), the founder of the Tendai school, felt the fifty-eight bodhisattva precepts would be more relevant and better adapted to the conditions of his times. As Paul Groner points out, however, although they were referred to by that school as the "Perfect Precepts", they were superseded by the esoteric precepts. And Annen (841–89), a Tendai master of Esoteric Buddhism, "argued that the esoteric precepts should never be violated but that other precepts, such as the *Brahma's Net Sutra* or Hinayana precepts, were expedients and could be readily violated if one were complying with the spirit of the esoteric precepts".[5]

Dogen (1200–53), one of the seminal thinkers and exponents of the Soto Zen school in Japan, reformed the bodhisattva precepts further by restructuring them into the Sixteen Great Bodhisattva Precepts. These are composed of the three refuges in the Buddha, Dharma and Sangha. To those are added the three fundamental precepts: to do no evil, to do good and to benefit all beings. They

21

are completed by the ten grave precepts, which are the ten major precepts of the *Brahma's Net Sutra*. Shinran (1173–1262), the founder of the Pure Land school in Japan, went even further and developed the idea of the "preceptless" precept.

The Tibetan Buddhist tradition is unlike that of Japan in that there are a greater number of bodhisattva vows than in the *Brahma's Net Sutra*. They consist of eighteen root vows and forty-six branch vows (a full list is given in the Appendix). Some of them are similar to the ones found in the *Brahma's Net Sutra*, but most are quite distinct.[6]

In terms of wisdom and compassion, the bodhisattva precepts of the *Brahma's Net Sutra* and the Tibetan Buddhist bodhisattva vows are basically similar, but on matters of detail they are quite different. This shows how various Buddhist traditions created ethics that fitted not only their particular cultural conditions and needs, but also the way they taught and practised the Dharma. It would be interesting to ponder and reflect on what kind of bodhisattva ethics could be created today to help us deal compassionately and wisely with this modern world, which though benefiting from technology and scientific progress is also deeply flawed, with too many ways to kill and hurt sentient beings and possibly to destroy our planet.

How the *Brahma's Net Sutra* came into being in China

China absorbed influences from various Buddhist schools over the centuries. Especially in the north, where the caravan routes were active for a long time, there was a constant flow of travellers who brought and passed on any new developments in the Buddhist faith in India and in the border regions. From 260 CE onwards there were also Chinese pilgrims going to the western regions in search of Buddhist texts. An Shih-Kao, one of the earliest translators into Chinese, was more interested in meditation texts and translated many Hinayana texts such as the *Agamas*. On the other hand, Chih-ch'an, a Scythian who arrived in Loyang around 167 CE, was mainly interested in the *Prajnaparamita* texts of the Mahayana tradition. Kumarajiva started to study the Hinayana tradition, but at the age of twenty, when he encountered Mahayana texts and teachings, he was so impressed by their profundity that he became a proponent of the Mahayana. However, this did not stop him from translating texts from both traditions and introducing Hinayana and Mahayana sutras into China. In the fourth and fifth century in China there was a great intellectual turmoil after the breakup of the country. Although both schools of Buddhism were introduced, the Chinese quickly showed a preference for the Mahayana with its richness of scope and philosophies. At that time the "Great Vehicle" was still in ferment, so that in China the Mahayana found a fertile terrain for further developments. In what follows I aim to show that the *Brahma's Net Sutra* is a good example of such original and indigenous developments.

Buddhism entered China in the first century CE via the great caravan route called the Silk Road that linked China with India. This route started in what is now Afghanistan, crossed over the Hindu Kush mountains, then followed the Takla-makan desert and ended in Tunhuang in north-western China. At that time, all along this caravan route there were Central Asian oasis kingdoms where Buddhism had flourished. (It seems that climatic changes led to the decline of these kingdoms.) Buddhism also came to China via the sea route in the second century, but this influence was not so strong. At the beginning, the main centres of Buddhism in China were Chang-an (now Sian) and the capital, Loyang, both situated in north-western China. Buddhist traders started to live there in the second century CE and Buddhist monks followed in their wake.

China was at a turning point in its history. Until then, Imperial Confucianism under the Han Dynasty (206 BCE–220 CE) had been the base for a strong and unified society centred on the Emperor, but attacks from within and from barbarians had weakened the state until China was divided into north and south. Non-Chinese conquered the north and ruled it from the fourth century until the end of the sixth. Southern China was ruled by Chinese dynasties. It is during this difficult period that Buddhism entered China and found fertile ground as the Chinese were less sure of the religious foundations of their society, Confucianism and Taoism. Buddhism seemed to offer a new way. By the time China was whole again (589), Buddhism had been accepted.

Buddhism, however, had to adapt to a radically different civilization. China was a society that attached great importance to scholarship. The imperial Chinese bureaucracy was made up of scholar officials who attained their ranks though examinations. First and foremost, Buddhist texts had to be translated from Central Asian languages or Sanskrit into Chinese. Chinese translations started in 150 CE and lasted until about 800 CE. At first there were two waves of translation activity. The earliest translations were difficult and rather flawed as the foreign monks did not really know Chinese and the Chinese translators did not know Sanskrit or Central Asian languages. These first translations were also strongly influenced by Taoist terms. Initially, Buddhism was seen as a type of Taoism from the western region. The need for more rigorous translations was recognized, as was the necessity of finding an appropriate Chinese vocabulary of Buddhist terms that would be accurate and meaningful. The second wave of translation (fifth and sixth century) was inaugurated by the arrival in China of Kumarajiva (343–413; alternatively 350–409), who is traditionally considered the translator of the *Brahma's Net Sutra*. It is said that Kumarajiva translated the bodhisattva precepts in 406 and that at that time three hundred of his disciples received them.

Kumarajiva is considered one of the greatest translators of all times. He was the son of an Indian father and a Kuchean princess who became a Buddhist nun after his birth (Kucha was one of the oasis kingdoms on the Silk Road). Kumarajiva became a Buddhist monk at the age of seven and travelled to Kashmir to study Buddhist texts with his mother. When he was twenty, he was fully ordained. He was an accomplished monk, well known for his extensive knowledge of the Buddhist sutras, and soon his fame grew and reached China. He was invited by the ruler to come to Ch'ang-an. Because of battles and disputes, however, he was detained in Liang-chou in north-western China for seventeen years, which gave him the opportunity to learn Chinese thoroughly. He finally arrived in Ch'ang-an in 402. Translation teams were assembled to improve the quality of the Buddhist texts available to the native Chinese population. As Kenneth Ch'en describes it:

> Kumarajiva would hold the text in his hand and proclaim its meaning in Chinese. He would explain the foreign text twice, taking great pains to select the exact phraseology to convey the meaning of the original. . . . In the meantime the audience of monks was discussing the meaning of the passages and passing judgement on the literary style. If there were any doubtful points in the Chinese reading, Kumarajiva checked them with the original. When no more changes were to be made, he then had the translation written in its final form.[7]

In this way Kumarajiva developed a new terminology that enabled him to translate Buddhist ideas with greater accuracy and clarity. His translations were also appreciated for their elegant style. The teams of Chinese specialists he formed created a large number of scholars and disciples who were well versed in the Buddhist canons and who started to write their own commentaries on the original Indian texts. An essential task was to make foreign Indian ideas understandable and religiously inspiring to a Chinese indigenous audience. Coherence was also needed. Buddhism arose around 500 BCE. By some 900 years later, around 400 CE, it had evolved considerably and embraced quite diverse teachings. There were also different monastic rules for various Buddhist schools.

In entering China, Indian Buddhism was challenged by different cultural and religious ideas and norms that were generally more pragmatic and secular. There was a very strong central power and a great respect for stable and harmonious human relationships. Essential was a mutual obligation within the family and between the ruler and the ruled. Buddhism did not seem applicable in practice or socio-politically effective. With its emphasis on impermanence, suffering, emptiness, karma and rebirth, equality and unity of its members, with precedence being based on time of ordination, Buddhism was quite revolutionary. The monastic ideal, with its celibacy and shaving of the head, seemed to contradict the basic tenets of filial piety, obedience and continued observance of the cult of the ancestors. Moreover, Buddhist monastics were expected to be totally outside the socio-political arena – exempt from state-labour, military service, payment of taxes and any supervision by the state. This was considered rather subversive and led to many conflicts and controversies.

Nevertheless, by 400 CE there were more than a thousand monasteries and ten thousand monks in the south. In the north too there were many monasteries, with monks and nuns who had to accept being supervised by state officials. However, this rapid and vast expansion seems to have led to repression, often instigated by Taoist and Confucian high officials. One of the worst early examples of repression occurred when advisers to the northern Wei emperor tried to block the advance of Buddhism by encouraging him to issue various decrees against Buddhism. This process started in 438 with a decree banning anyone under fifty from becoming a monk, followed by a decree in 444 that forbade anyone to support monks privately; it culminated in 446 with an edict that all stupas and sutras be burnt and all monks and nuns killed. Not all these decrees were implemented, but many sutras and temples were destroyed and a large number of monks and nuns were executed. By 454 all the people involved in this repression had died and the new actors on the political stage allowed and supported a revival of Buddhism.

An original Chinese Buddhist scripture

All these explanations and historical data are essential to understand the context in which the *Brahma's Net Sutra* was created. From 400 CE there started to appear in China what I shall call "original Chinese Buddhist sutras", often referred to as apocrypha by scholars. These texts were created to respond to the needs of the Chinese people and to help them benefit from the depth of the Buddhist tradition. These original Chinese Buddhist sutras are composed of elements from traditional Buddhist sutras mixed with relevant and essential Chinese ideas. The *Brahma's Net Sutra* is a good example of this kind of text.

After lengthy research, scholars have recently come to agree that although the *Brahma's Net Sutra* was traditionally assumed to be the tenth chapter of a lost Indian text translated in 406 CE by

Kumarajiva, it is actually a text composed in China between 440 and 480 CE. One of the main pieces of evidence supporting this hypothesis is the repeated appearance in the text of the two Chinese characters for "filial piety and obedience" (fifteen times in all). Only original Chinese Buddhist sutras contain these characters, which occur three times in quick succession at the beginning of the text in "The Origin of the Bodhisattva Precepts" (as I explain in the notes, I translate these two characters as "devoted", which works better for a modern rendering): "This entails being devoted [filial and obedient] to the Three Jewels, one's teachers and one's parents. It is the Dharma of being devoted [filial and obedient] to the true way. Such devotion [filial piety and obedience] is called both *sila* [ethics, precepts] and *vinaya* [discipline, control]." Here we have filial pity towards not only parents but also teachers and, most important, to the Three Jewels. By being filial to these three, one is also filial to the true way (Tao). As used here, the word "way" (Tao) is a fundamental Taoist concept. The author is therefore using terms with which the Chinese are familiar, and this makes them feel more comfortable with the text. Finally, filial piety is equated with the precepts that follow.

The author seems to be stressing that Buddhist ethical conduct is compatible with, if not equal to, the concepts of filial piety and obedience that are the basis of Confucian ethics. This was one of the major stumbling blocks for Buddhists. Again and again they were attacked by the Confucians for not only failing to stress filial piety and obedience but also going against it. If, however, one looks at the early Buddhist sutras known as *Agamas* in China, the Buddha does advocate respect and support for one's parents. For example, in the translation from the Pali in the *Sigalaka Sutta* (*Advice to Laypeople*), the Buddha says:

> There are five ways in which a son should minister to his mother and father. ... Having been supported by them, I will support them, I will perform their duties for them. I will keep up the family tradition. I will be worthy of my heritage. After my parents' death I will distribute gifts on their behalf.[8]

This text was rendered into Chinese by different translators, with some variations. Here, for example, are two versions of the five ways mentioned above as they appear in two different Chinese translations. One version stipulates that a son should "1) support his parents, 2) rise early to order the servants to prepare breakfast for the parents, 3) not cause his parents worry, 4) seek a doctor immediately if his parents are ill, 5) reflect on the parents' love for him". The other requires him "1) to increase the material wealth, 2) to manage all the business of [his] parents, 3) to respond immediately to their wishes, 4) not to go contrary to their desires, 5) to present all their private possessions to them".⁹

It is noticeable that the earlier Pali version is more general and that the Chinese versions start to make these injunctions more specific and practical. This sutra was translated many times because it fitted with the Chinese ethos. Although respect and gratitude for parents are mentioned in early Buddhist texts, it is not the main thrust of the Buddha's message; it is only part of the duty and responsibility of a disciple of the Buddha to be respectful and kind within all relationships. And this is how the Chinese Buddhists countered the Confucians' accusations, trying to show that Buddhist filial piety is actually more universal than Confucian filial piety, which is centred on one's family.

On the other hand, in the thirteenth secondary precept, about "not slandering others", the author has inserted: "He should always nurture a devoted [filial and obedient] and compassionate attitude towards his parents, brothers and sisters and all the other six kinds of family relatives." Here the text is in complete accord with the Confucian notion of filial piety. In the *Brahma's Net Sutra*, the author seems to have two aims regarding filial piety: to conform to Confucian notions and at the same time to add an extra and more attractive Buddhist value to it.

For example, in the first major bodhisattva precept, it is said: "It is the duty of a bodhisattva to be always compassionate and devoted [filial and obedient] towards others." In the ninth major precept we find: "He should always present a compassionate and devout [filial and obedient] state of mind." Here we see how in the *Brahma's Net Sutra* filial piety is associated with compassion, indicating that it is not a self-contained duty but is complementary to the desire to save all beings. This is a definite departure from ordinary Chinese filial piety. In the tenth major precept it is associated with being faithful. In the seventeenth secondary precept it is again associated with compassion as in the twenty-ninth precept, where it is extended to cultivating a wholesome occupation. In the twenty-first precept the notion of filial piety is used in a way that could be thought contrary to Confucian filial piety: "to take revenge on someone who has killed (even one's parents) by killing him is not in accordance with the principle of devotion [filial piety]". From the Confucian point of view the killing of a parent or the king should be avenged. Here, however, because of the Buddhist context which includes the concept of rebirth, and cause and effect, one is encouraged not to kill in revenge. It is thought that such actions would perpetuate the cycle of killing in future lives. So again, Buddhism brings a larger and more universal aspect to filial piety and ethical conduct, instead of just considering the here and now and concerning oneself only with one's family.

In the twenty-eighth secondary precept, filial piety is actually used to forbid individual invitation to the monks: "to do so is not the way of true devotion [filial piety]". In this case, the author extends the concept of filial piety to cover respect for the proper way of running the community of monks, whose status is considered to be contrary to filial piety because they are celibate and do not continue the family line. Perhaps the author is trying to show that, in Buddhism, filial piety underpins every action, even outside invitations.

In the first secondary precept, the bodhisattva is instructed to greet all teachers and fellow practitioners with a devout (filial) mind. Here the whole Buddhist community becomes worthy of filial piety, thus becoming one's family. In a Korean Buddhist monastery it is indeed so: one's preceptor becomes one's father, one's preceptor's preceptor one's grandfather, and so on.

In the thirty-fifth secondary precept a bodhisattva is told always to make vows to be devoted to his parents and his teachers. Here we notice that the parents come first. This could be to fit Chinese standards, but it could also be related to the fact that one is devoted first to one's parents, and those who become monks or nuns will then become devoted to their teachers; in this way, teachers and parents are made equal. In the forty-sixth secondary precept, one is encouraged to have the same filial piety towards one's teacher as towards one's parents, again suggesting the equality of teachers and parents. Finally, in the forty-eighth precept to break one of the precepts is considered to show a lack of filial piety.

Buddhism and the state

Historically, it is interesting to note in several of the secondary precepts the mention of secular authorities. The first secondary precept states: "When a disciple of the Buddha attains the position of a king or a *chakravatin*, or when he is appointed to a government post, he must first receive the bodhisattva precepts." The author supports a connection between the state and Buddhism, and it was during the Northern Wei that Buddhism and the state were very close. This could explain the repeated injunctions against using any association with high office for the benefit of oneself at the expense of others. The title of precept 17, "Do not beg for and try to obtain things by relying on the authorities", could not be more explicit. Precept 23 discourages teachers from being proud and unhelpful on account of close acquaintance with a king, prince or government official. In precept 32 one is enjoined not to use influence with government offices to deprive others of their possessions; a similar injunction is expressed in precept 48.

But this connection with high office must be expressed with the proper reverence. In the first secondary precept the sentence above is immediately followed by the notion that the authorities must show reverence to teachers and co-religionists. And in the middle of the fortieth secondary precept it is stated very clearly: "A person who has renounced the household life must not bow to the king, his parents, or any of the six kinds of close relatives, nor to spirits." So the author seems to want connection with the state, but on Buddhism's terms. The outsider and elevated status of the monastics must remain true. Three precepts at least focus on the proper order or the proper place. Precept 37 states that "the reciter [of the precepts] must be seated in a high place and those listening in a lower place". Precept 46 reiterates that, even when among nobility, one does not expound the Dharma standing but must be seated high up. And the whole of precept 38 is about not disregarding "the order of 'high' and 'low'", in this instance meaning that one sits according to the date of one's ordination and not according to rank, age or status. This was very revolutionary for Chinese society.

The eleventh precept is interesting because it seems to want to pre-empt one of the worries of the state in relation to Buddhists: that an unregulated group of religious could create opportunities for organizing rebellions. It states categorically that a bodhisattva should not become a military envoy, set foot in an army camp, and most particularly should not engage in rebellious or seditious acts.

In terms of the repression of 446, precepts 31 and 47 are illuminating. In precept 31 there is mention of the selling of monastics, of making them become slaves or servants of government officials, and it is stated that one should redeem images and sutras and rescue monastics – all of which suggests that such things had happened. The whole of precept 47 seems to be addressing such repression without mentioning it by name and with the intent of ensuring that it does not occur again. This precept, entitled "Do not establish regulations on the basis of an erroneous law", states that

> a king, a prince, a government official or a member of the fourfold assembly ... must never ... destroy the Buddhadharma and the precepts by creating erroneous laws and taking disciplinary actions to limit the activities of the fourfold assembly. Thus he must never obstruct someone from leaving the household life in order to cultivate the way. Nor must he ever prevent the making of images of the Buddha or the construction of stupas, or hinder the copying of sutras and *vinayas*. He must not maintain an administration which places regulations and restrictions on the activities of the sangha. Neither must he spread such customs as having bodhisattvas who are monks stand on the ground while laypeople are seated higher up, or treat the monks like common soldiers or slaves serving their master. When a bodhisattva is worthy of receiving the offerings of all people, how could he ever become the servant of a government official?

The presence of such social and political considerations in the bodhisattva precepts shows how much Buddhist monastics had to adapt to survive on Chinese soil. In India the monastics were supported by laypeople but were separate from society. In China, however, this could not entirely be the case. The emperor and the government could not accept an independent body in their midst, so they had to exercise strict control and supervision of the Buddhist monastics. The numbers of monks and nuns were regulated and somewhat restricted by the ordination certificates bestowed by the state. In order to be ordained officially one had to go through examinations conducted by the government authorities. Moreover, the monks and the nuns had to be registered with the civil authorities, something that had never happened in India.

Some scholars think that it took two centuries for the *Brahma's Net Sutra* to be adopted by all Buddhists in China and to become the fundamental text it is now. Thereafter it would be the basis for the ethical life of the laity and the monastics in China, Korea and Japan. It is an example of the love, compassion and universality that Buddhism brought to China and that had such a profound impact on Chinese culture and society by making possible the idea of a welfare society. At that time, with the approval of the government, Buddhist temple communities took the lead in taking care of such charitable activities as the building of hospitals, dispensaries, rest houses and homes for the aged. They also participated in projects benefiting the whole community, for instance the building of roads and bridges, the digging of wells and the planting of shady trees along the roadside.

The path of compassion

Early on in Korea I realized and experienced clearly the essential connection between compassion and ethics. Often we were told the story of the monk and the flea – how in ancient times when a monk found a flea at the beginning of winter, he could not let it outside but kept it warm and fed it over the winter and released it only when warm spring came. In the summer in Korea there were flies and mosquitoes, so we devised a method of catching them with a glass and a postcard in order to release them outside the room. We found that we could not kill them intentionally, because we knew that they too lived and wanted to continue to live and also possessed the Buddha nature. We felt they had as much right to life as we did. It might be harder to do this in a tropical country.

Many of the Bodhisattva precepts are about not harming either oneself or others, or animals. The first major precept is to "Refrain from taking life". It points out in great detail that one should not kill or cause someone else to kill, or kill in a roundabout way, or create the cause or conditions, or the means to kill. It is an exhaustive list that makes us reflect on the many ways in which we might cause harm. We might not kill other people or any living creatures, but do we cause them harm in any other way? And if we cause them harm, how do we do it? Do we do it in a roundabout way so that we do not feel responsible for it? Do we create the causes and conditions for causing harm needlessly? These precepts show us that wisdom and compassion help us to reflect on our actions and intentions. Then the precept explains why we should not kill, and that is because the duty of a bodhisattva is to be always compassionate and to lead others to liberation.

There are several precepts that investigate what it means to be non-harming as a result of a compassionate attitude. The third major precept, which encourages proper sexual behaviour, states that the reason for doing so is that otherwise perverted, indecent, indiscriminate sexual behaviour would obliterate compassion. When overcome by lustful thoughts or feelings, can one reflect on what would be the compassionate course for all involved in that moment? As this precept reminds us, "It is the duty of a bodhisattva always to present a state of mind which conforms to the Buddha-nature and to lead others to liberation by teaching them the pure Dharma."

The third secondary precept encourages vegetarianism on the grounds that to eat the flesh of animals would destroy great compassion and kindness and the seed of the Buddha nature. To this day, monasteries and nunneries in China and Korea are completely vegetarian. Because laypeople found it more difficult to be fully vegetarian, six specified fasting or vegetarian days a month were created as well as three special months of abstinence (i.e. times when animal food is avoided).

The fourteenth precept is concerned with lighting destructive fires at certain times of the year at the risk of causing harm to living creatures. In Korea, the monastery's fields were burnt only during the depth of the winter when all living creatures were dormant and out of harm's way. The twentieth precept requires us to save the lives of living creatures and to set loose those about to be killed. To this day in China and Korea, Buddhists will go to the market to buy live animals, like fish and birds, to release them in the wild. In ancient times in Chinese monasteries there were even spacious individual pens for the different animals that laypeople had bought and brought to finish their days in peaceful surroundings.

The tenth and the thirty-second precepts concern themselves with not keeping or selling implements for killing, such as swords and clubs; thus they relate to the clause about creating the means or the causes and conditions for harming or killing. Once in the kitchen of a prosecutor in Canada, I was presented with the main weapon used in serious offences in that region: a kitchen knife! It was a sobering experience. In the hands of a peaceful person, a knife is very useful; in the hands of someone in the grip of rage, it is extremely dangerous.

The precepts also look at one of the psychological and emotional conditions for causing harm: anger. The ninth major precept urges us to refrain from being angry or quarrelsome and encourages us to be kind and compassionate. It points out that as a result of anger one might abuse an animal or even hit an inanimate object. Human beings seem not to have changed much since ancient times: we may still find ourselves kicking a car tyre or thumping a computer key-board. The twenty-first secondary precept even argues against repaying anger with anger and taking revenge. As an example, it singles out venting one's anger on servants; nowadays this could apply to people working in the public sector. Who has not got hot under the collar and felt vengeful and short-tempered when faced with a representative of industry or government? This again is considered to be abandoning a compassionate mind.

Another contributory factor in inflicting harm that is investigated is alcohol. It is considered more serious to sell it (fifth major precept) than to drink it oneself (second secondary precept). In the former precept it is pointed out that alcohol is a conditional factor in committing negative and harmful actions. It can lead people into confusion, which goes against the duty of a bodhisattva to cultivate wisdom in the minds of living beings.

These precepts help us to reflect not just on what is harmful but also on the pursuit of positive and beneficial activities. The thirty-first secondary precept asks us to rescue people from difficulties, and in the ninth we are encouraged to care well and provide for someone who is sick as if for the Buddha himself. It is pointed out that one should not fail to nurse or give assistance because of dislike and resentment. On reflection we may be reminded that we are often uncomfortable visiting someone ill in hospital, perhaps because we are not at ease in hospitals or because our friend is diminished by illness. But if we cultivate a wise and compassionate heart, we realize that, while our friend is suffering all the time, we are uncomfortable for only thirty minutes or an hour. I find when faced with pain or distress that compassion can dissolve any unease in the presence of the person who is ill.

In my youth I had been an anarchist and so in general was not enamoured of the banking system. Once, when I was changing money in a bank in Korea after becoming a nun, the cashier gave me back too much money. At first I was tempted to rush out with my windfall. This was quickly followed by the compassionate thought that I could not take the money because the cashier would suffer for his error, so I returned the money and told him of his mistake. As the second major precept, "Refrain from taking what is not given", tries to explain at length, it is not just plain and simple stealing that is referred to. It is again looking at the means, the causes and conditions and the roundabout ways in which one could achieve the aim of obtaining something that is not freely or consciously given. We are reminded that "the duty of a bodhisattva is to make others joyful and happy by always presenting a state of mind which conforms to the Buddha-nature". We refrain from stealing, not because it is illegal but because to do so would be contrary to the Buddha-nature and awakening.

There are three more precepts that deal with material possessions and livelihood. The twelfth secondary precept is about refraining from doing business with evil intent; the seventeenth is about not trying to extort money or goods with threats of violence or by corruption with the help of well-placed people. The twenty-ninth concerns not holding an unwholesome occupation with evil intent and for the sake of gain, because to do any of these things is contrary to a mind of compassion. These precepts are very practical and are intended to cover all aspects of life. They are asking of us: "What does it mean to live an ethical and compassionate life fully and extensively?"

Intention is an important aspect of ethics that is mentioned in many precepts. The words "intentionally" and "deliberately" are often used. Whether something is done intentionally or accidentally makes a difference. It is therefore essential to look into one's own mind and heart and to question one's motives for acting in a particular way. If an accident repeats itself often enough to cause harm, it would be important to investigate the conditions and the states of mind that gave rise to the action, and to its result.

Some precepts are about how we communicate and express a compassionate mind and heart verbally, and what would be contrary to that. This is investigated in depth from many different angles. For example, the fourth major precept is to "refrain from telling lies". It is suggested that one should not convey the impression that one saw something that one did not see (or vice versa) through physical gesture or mental intention: even if one is not lying in words, one might do so through gesture or in the mind. We are being made aware of subtle aspects of communication. It is not only through words that we express ourselves. We must also consider what impressions we convey, and what is the intention behind them. These precepts are not only about our actions but also about our underlying intentions, and they require us to be fully alert to both.

There are three precepts that deal with slandering. The seventh major precept is interesting because it suggests an exchange of self for other as in the compassionate practice found in Shantideva. It points out that one should not praise oneself while slandering others, the reason being that "the duty of a bodhisattva is to take upon himself the slander directed towards others, to transfer whatever is unpleasant to himself and to give whatever good to others". This is one of the challenges of compassion, to let go of self-centredness to become other-centred. We are often afraid of other-centredness because we feel that others will take advantage. In my experience the opposite happens: when we become more open to and more genuinely concerned for others, they will reciprocate, and in that way self-centredness can start to diminish on both sides. By living according to other-centredness rather than self-preservation we show that it is possible to do so and that it leads to harmony and creativity.

The eighth major precept explores the connection between reviling someone and miserliness – how we should not be miserly in general and should try to give whatever is requested of us if we can. This precept points out that an ungenerous attitude can stop us from extending ourselves for others. It might also make us think harshly of someone in order to avoid giving anything to that person. When we pass beggars in the street, it is salutary to be aware of any negative attitude we may harbour towards them that will excuse us from giving even the little they ask of us who have so much more. Finally, in the thirteenth precept one is asked not to slander someone baselessly and with evil intent. Although we might consider that we do not slander others in general, what do we do when we gossip? How do we talk about people behind their backs? Are we positive and constructive or rather the reverse? Do we contribute to creating harmony and understanding or do we do the opposite? Here it is pointed out that slandering others is not beneficial towards nurturing a compassionate attitude because it causes suffering.

The main message of the *Brahma's Net Sutra* and of the bodhisattva precepts that can help us in our modern life is that the path of ethics is expressed as compassion in action and the path of compassion is based on an ethical attitude.

Compassion in action

In Korea and Taiwan there are many examples of monks, nuns and laypeople trying to live and act as bodhisattvas. For example, Venerable Cheng Yen is a Taiwanese Chinese Buddhist nun who started the Tzu Chi Foundation in 1966. She is the abbess of a small nunnery and the instigator of a wide programme to provide medical services to all, especially the needy. Starting with five nuns and fifty cents of daily savings from thirty households, Venerable Cheng Yen has established hospitals, medical colleges and research centres in Taiwan. The foundation also helps people struck by disasters all over the world. To this day, the nuns derive no personal benefit from the enormous amount of money they raise, and they work daily to earn their keep. Venerable Cheng Yen encourages her followers to earn money to give to others: to use what they need for themselves and give as much as they can of what is left. She says that money is a tool and one must be careful not to be used by it.

In Korea, Venerable Kwangou is a senior nun in charge of a large educational centre in a suburb of Seoul, the capital of South Korea. Before becoming the director of this centre, Venerable Kwangou had created a modern Buddhist temple in Seoul to respond to the demands and conditions of ordinary people. She believes that as a Buddhist one must do bodhisattva actions and be productive in one's own life while teaching and transforming others. When the city council built this educational centre in a suburb to help the youth of the area, they asked the main Buddhist order to take charge of it. In turn the order thought that nuns would be better at guiding and helping the youth. Venerable Kwangou was elected director of this centre by the Buddhist Nuns' Association. She told me that people really enjoyed the youth centre because there were so many activities at very low fees. The elderly are allowed in free. They can come twice a week to learn swimming, which helps them relax, and they return much happier to their families, who live stressful lives in the high-rise buildings nearby. At the beginning Venerable Kwangou took charge of the centre reluctantly, but now she realizes that this too is a way to perform bodhisattva actions by creating harmony and happiness among people, young and old.

Another example of a contemporary bodhisattva in action is Pang Kwihi, a Korean Buddhist writer who is confined to a wheelchair because her lower body did not develop. She is a successful novelist, Buddhist lecturer and scriptwriter. Originally she wanted to be a doctor, but in the 1970s it was difficult for disabled people to go to university in Korea and she was able only to join a Buddhist university. She started to study Buddhism without faith in it but quickly realized that the Buddha's message of awakening and compassion was very inspiring and she became attracted to its practices. Now she tries to apply the Buddha's teachings in her daily life. Whenever she meets difficulties she thinks of something the Buddha said to help her handle them. She wrote a novel called *Rahula* – one meaning of the word is "handicap" – because she wanted to investigate what restricts people in their lives and what liberates them. She set up the Association of Disabled Writers and founded a literature magazine to publish their work and thus make them known and help them earn respect and a livelihood.

The text

The *Brahma's Net Sutra* is seen as one of the texts that contributed to the development of the idea and practice of repentance. Ceremonies of repentance, personal or communal, and the practice of repentance, private or communal, are two representative elements of Chinese and Korean Buddhism. In the fifth secondary precept, one is instructed to encourage others to repent if they have committed faults. In the forty-first secondary precept it is stated that one must repent if one transgresses one of the ten major precepts.

Repentance, purity and the precepts are inextricably linked. In the Preparation it is clear that the assembly has to be pure before it can receive the precepts, so first the reciter asks about the purity of the assembly. Then, in the preamble proper, one is questioned about one's state of virtue, and anyone who has committed non-virtuous acts must repent. The repentance is considered an active principle of the path as it is equated with a peaceful mind. Conversely, failure to repent strengthens the power of the negative tendency. At the root of repentance there is an awareness that one has committed negative deeds that hurt oneself and others and thus will be opposed and detrimental to a mind of compassion and wisdom.

There are a few precepts about seeking and requesting instructions, and asking questions about, reading and learning the Dharma well. Besides showing how an interest in scholarship may have been highly esteemed in Chinese society, this indicates that wisdom and knowledge about the teachings of the Buddha are essential components of the path. But the main importance of learning in terms of the bodhisattva path is that one can then help and transform others. Thus there are also many precepts related to teaching and transforming others. One should not force oneself or the Buddhist teaching on others but should always be ready to teach if this can help others and benefit them. The Buddha was very clear about this. He gave the injunction that if a disciple of Buddha is questioned about the Dharma, he or she should always respond; but if someone does not ask anything, you should let them go on their way in peace.

Renunciation is considered a main element of the Hinayana tradition. And the Mahayana did not reject the notion of renunciation but in some ways reinvigorated it. In the first secondary precept one is told that one must be willing to sell one's body, country, sons, daughters, jewels or possessions to provide food for one's teachers and companions in the way. In the sixteenth secondary precept one again is asked to give one's body, this time to starving animals; this is in emulation of the sacrifice of the Buddha in the *Jataka* tale mentioned earlier.

Associated with renunciation is the notion of cultivating certain ascetic practices that also came from the Hinayana and are mentioned in the sixteenth precept in terms of instructing others about them. The thirty-seventh secondary precept explains in detail how to perform itinerant ascetic practices. These practices seemed mainly directed towards the monastics as they are connected in this precept with their meditation retreats. One of the characteristics of this ethical text, however, is that it is addressed both to monastics and to lay followers. Most precepts apply to both categories, although some apply only to one or the other. This could lead to confusion, but it could also be read as bringing the experience of both groups to the ethical endeavour and so make both aware of the tasks to be accomplished in each category. Hospitality among both groups and towards each other is also a quality and a service that is strongly encouraged in the bodhisattva precepts. Many precepts refer to welcoming guests and providing them with food or anything else they might need.

The *Brahma's Net Sutra* includes various cultural aspects among its diverse elements. For example, in the fourth secondary precept there is an injunction against eating pungent vegetables like garlic and onions. To this day in monasteries in China and Korea, no onion or garlic is cooked or eaten. This practice came from the yogic tradition of India, such vegetables being thought to inflame the humours and provoke lust or anger. In the thirty-third precept one is enjoined not to look at unwholesome things. What is described is typical of fifth-century China: games of "pitching arrows into a pot" and divination made with mirrors made of claws! Although at one level this text is universal, at another level it helps us connect and empathize with people in fifth-century China in a direct and intimate way. Could we create such an ethical text that might be used by and help future generations while clearly showing them how we live now? Approached in this way, the *Brahma's Net Sutra* could help us to reflect and devise ethics for our modern times.

The translation

The title of the sutra seems to derive from a passage at the beginning of the text where the Buddha refers to a parasol that is made from Brahma's net.[10] There he makes a comparison between the holes of the net and the infinite differences in his teachings: "All the numberless worlds are similar to the holes in this net. Each individual world is unlike any of the others. There are infinite differences between them. The teachings of the Buddha are also like this." In Buddhism, Brahma is understood as a worldly deity inhabiting the realm of form. In China, Brahma became also the symbol for India, the land where the Buddha was born. It was at the request of Brahma that the Buddha started to teach after his awakening.

This translation of the *Brahma's Net Sutra* is made up of five sections:

> The Preparation
> The Origin of the Bodhisattva Precepts
> The Ten Major and the Forty-Eight Secondary Bodhisattva Precepts
> The Conclusion
> The Apology and the Dedication

The first section is the preparatory ceremony before the bodhisattva precepts themselves are received. The first part of the Preparation consists in ceremonial chants that are recited by the whole assembly if it is present at such times. These are regular Buddhist chants like the paying of homage to the Three Jewels: the Buddhas, the Dharma (teaching) and the Sangha (community of Buddhist disciples).

This homage chant is followed by the offering of incense. In Buddhist ceremonies in Korea, incense, water and candles are offered on the altar. At the time of the Buddha in India two and a half thousand years ago, people used to sacrifice animals at special ceremonies. In the *Kutadanta Sutta*[11] the Buddha stated that it was much better to offer a bloodless sacrifice of butter or honey, or other such items that would not cause animals to be harmed or killed. This has always been observed in the Chinese and Korean Buddhist tradition.

The chants are followed by the actual ceremony of purification in which the reciter, the precept master who is in charge of making sure the precepts are kept in the monastery, addresses the assembly

on his own as it is stated in the thirty-seventh secondary bodhisattva precept. Part of his task at the time of the ceremony is to
check that everyone is pure and so able to receive the precepts. He
will therefore question and cross-examine the assembly several
times. I have presented this part of the text in such a way that readers will be able to feel for themselves how the *Brahma's Net Sutra*
is experienced and lived to this day in Korea.

The second section, "The Origin of the Bodhisattva Precepts as
Taught in the *Brahma's Net Sutra*", is a short passage outlining the
history of the text, the life of the Buddha and the importance of
these precepts. It is in two forms, prose followed by verse: a standard formulation found in Buddhist sutras, with the verses para-
phrasing the prose and expanding it as in this text. Here this
section is much shorter than in other Chinese recensions of the
Brahma's Net Sutra. De Groot in his French translation of the
Brahma's Net Sutra in 1893 mentioned that, although most texts
in China had the shorter version, he was able to find some with the
longer version. He noted that the language of this section in the
longer texts was more elaborate, philosophical and abstruse than
the third section, that of the bodhisattva precepts, which he felt
was written in a simple and direct style. The text as presented here
is the one used in the temple of Songgwang in Korea.

The third section of the *Brahma's Net Sutra* consists of the ten
major and the forty-eight secondary bodhisattva precepts. This is
followed by a Conclusion that is similar in tone to "The Origin of
the Bodhisattva Precepts": it has the same style of language, being
flowery and philosophical, again with both prose and verse. The
fifth section constitutes the end of the ceremony, with an apology
to the assembly from the lone reciter and a verse of dedication
chanted by the whole assembly.

This translation of the bodhisattva precepts has been prepared
mainly from the *Profound Mirror of the Bodhisattva* (*Posal
Hyongam*; compiled, edited and rendered into vernacular Korean
by Venerable Chaun Sunim, 1977). The sections of instruction at
the beginning and end of the text were taken from the *Supplementary Volume to the Brahma's Net Sutra* (*Pommang Kyong*

Kwon Ha; compiled, edited and translated into vernacular Korean by Venerable Chongil Sunim, 1979). Throughout, reference was made to *Clear Reading of the Ceremony of Purification for the Bodhisattva Precepts* (*Posal Kye P'osal Namgsong Pon*; compiled, edited and translated into the vernacular by Venerable Ilta Sunim, 1983). The translation was made on the basis of the Korean vernacular texts, with reference to the Chinese original. For the clarification of difficult passages, Venerable Popchong Sunim was consulted. The text was first edited by Stephen Batchelor in 1983. Recently I have reworked this translation and compared it with others, in French and English, listed in the Bibliography.

The Bodhisattva Precepts

I

Preparation

Paying homage to the Three Jewels

We wholeheartedly bow to all the Buddhas of the universe throughout the ten directions.
We wholeheartedly bow to the sacred Dharma of the universe throughout the ten directions.
We wholeheartedly bow to the noble Sangha of the universe throughout the ten directions.
The ceremony of purification will now take place by means of the recitation of the precepts.
Our sole wish is that the Three Jewels will bear witness to this.

Offering incense

May these clouds of fragrant incense entirely pervade the universe throughout the ten directions

Thus adorning all Buddha-worlds with their inexhaustible scent
And establishing within us the way of the bodhisattvas
So that we will be able to realize the exquisite fragrance of the Tathagatas.

recite three times:
Homage to the great Bodhisattva "Fragrance-Cloud-Canopy"!

Invoking the Buddha's name

recite three times:
Homage to Rocana Buddha,
Lord of the teaching of the *Brahma's Net Sutra*.

Opening the text of the sutra

In one hundred or one thousand aeons it is very difficult to meet
The unsurpassable, profound and wonderful Dharma of the
   Buddhas.
Being now able to hear it, see it and receive it,
May we come to understand the true meaning of the Tathagata!

THE CEREMONY OF PURIFICATION

The reciter mounts the raised Dharma seat and proceeds to address the assembly.

I humbly present to you my salutations. Since you have requested to recite these precepts, I will now respectfully do so. In the case of my making mistakes, I hope that all of you gathered will compassionately correct my errors.

Taking refuge in and paying respect to the Three Jewels

Let us take refuge in Rocana Buddha and all the adamantine Buddhas of the ten directions! Let us pay our respects to the future Buddha Maitreya, the Lord of all Commentaries! Shortly the three ethical principles for the accumulating [of virtue] will be recited. All bodhisattvas gathered here should listen well to them. Why? Because the ethical precepts are like a brilliant lamp which can disperse the darkness of the night. They are like a most precious mirror which is able to reflect the Dharma in its entirety. They are like a most valuable gem which frees one from poverty and endows one with wealth.

Having renounced the world in order to attain Buddhahood, the Dharma alone is the supreme means to attain one's goal. Therefore, it is essential that all bodhisattvas diligently protect and uphold this Dharma.

Encouraging the practice of virtue

Venerable Ones! This is the time during the three-month winter and summer retreat when we all have to gather here together. A certain amount of this retreat period has already passed and only a certain amount still remains. Yet old age and death are close at hand and the teaching of the Buddha is in the process of disappearing. All of us, therefore – monks and nuns, laymen and laywomen – should dedicate ourselves wholeheartedly to the realization of the way. Why? Because all the Buddhas, having likewise applied themselves wholeheartedly, have thereby realized the true, supreme, unsurpassable awakening. What better thing could there be to accomplish than this? While you are still in good health, you should listen well and make a great effort [to realize this goal]. But although you should be cultivating the way of virtue, why, instead of doing this, do you just calmly wait for old age to arrive? What is it that you intend to enjoy [then]? Today is already passing quickly by. In the same way is your very life on the way to destruction. We are like fish in a rapidly diminishing pool of water. What kind of happiness is awaiting us?

Questioning the assembly

Q: Is the assembly now gathered?
A: It is now gathered.
Q: Is the assembly in harmony?
A: The assembly is in harmony.
Q: Why has the assembly gathered together in harmony?
A: It has done so in order to recite the precepts and conduct the ceremony of purification.
Q: Is there anyone among you who has not received the precepts or who is impure?

A: There is no one among us who has not received the precepts or
   who is impure.
Q: Is there anyone who was unable to come and excused himself
   on grounds of his being pure?
A: There is no one who was unable to come and excused himself
   on grounds of his being pure.
Now please fold your hands in prayer.

Preamble to [the recitation of] the bodhisattva precepts

Sons of the Buddha! Please listen with an earnest mind. I shall now
recite the preamble to the precepts as expounded by the Buddha.
Now that the assembly has gathered, please quietly pay attention
[to these words]. If you are aware of evil deeds within yourselves,
then you must repent. If you repent, then you will be at peace with
yourselves. But if you do not repent, the force of the evil deeds will
become even stronger. If you have no evil deeds, then just remain
quiet. I will take that to mean that you are pure.

Monks and nuns, laymen and laywomen! Please listen carefully.
For those during the later period of the Dharma, after the Buddha
has entered Nirvana, it has been taught that they must pay respect
to the *Pratimoksha*. The *Pratimoksha* is nothing other than the
precepts themselves. If you keep the precepts, it will be like seeing
the light of a fire in a dark place. It will be like a poor man finding
a jewel. It will be like a sick person being restored to health. It will
be like a prisoner being released. It will be like the return of someone who has wandered far from home.

Know that these precepts are a teacher for all of you. Even if the
Buddha were among us today, this would still be the case. But it is
difficult to give rise to a mind which is afraid of evil deeds. And it
is even more difficult to give rise to a mind which is intent on
virtue. For this reason it is said in the sutra: "Do not treat little
evils lightly and claim that no misfortune will result from them.
For although drops of water are very small, one by one they will
come to fill a large vessel." Even the evil performed in a single
moment can cause one to fall into the Avici hell. Once you have

lost this human body, it will be hard to find it again even in the next ten thousand aeons. Youth is like a swiftly galloping horse which soon disappears. Human life slips by even faster than water cascading from a high mountain. Although we can say we are alive today, we cannot guarantee that we will survive until tomorrow.

With a steady mind apply yourselves with diligence and do not indulge in idle thoughts. During the night-time observe your mind closely and think of the Three Jewels. Do not just spend your time in vain. For if you tire yourselves out with futile activities, you will only come to regret it in the future. Each one of you should, without fail, practise in accordance with the Dharma as it is stated in these precepts.

Cross-examination of the assembly

Noble Ones! Today is the —— day. The ceremony of purification is taking place and the precepts are about to be recited. Please listen with all your heart. Will those with evil deeds please show yourselves and will those without any remain silent. Since you all remain silent, I take it to mean that you are all pure. Thus I can proceed to recite the precepts. Now that the preamble to the bodhisattva precepts has been expounded, I must put the following questions to you virtuous ones:

Are those of you gathered here pure?
Are those of you gathered here pure?
Are those of you gathered here pure?

Since you remain silent, I take it to mean that you are indeed pure. Please continue to dwell in this state of purity.

II

The Origin of the Bodhisattva Precepts as Taught in the Brahma's Net Sutra

translated by
the Tripitaka Master of the Chin Dynasty,
the Venerable Kumarajiva

It came to pass that the Buddha, having first appeared in the world called "Lotus Platform Treasury", went to the East and entered the palace of Lord Indra. There he taught the sutra entitled "The Conversion of the Host of Mara". It was after this that he was born in our world of Jambudvipa, in the land of Kapila.

He announced, "My mother was called Maya and my father Suddhodana. My name was Siddhartha. Having left home, I practised rigorously for seven years. At the age of thirty I realized enlightenment. From then on I was called Shakyamuni Buddha. From the time I sat on the 'Diamond Lotus Radiant King' throne in the tranquil Bodhimandala until I reached the palace of Mahesvara, king of the celestials, I progressively taught [the Dharma] in ten different places."

Then the Buddha observed the parasol which was made from the net of Lord Brahma and declared, "All the numberless worlds are similar to the holes in this net. Each individual world is unlike any of the others. There are infinite differences between them." The teachings of the Buddha are also like this.

I have appeared in this world eight hundred times. During the entire time which has elapsed from my sitting on the throne of enlightenment until my reaching the place of Mahesvara, I have been concisely yet fully expounding the fundamental words of Dharma [literally "Mind-Ground Dharma Discourse"] for the benefit of many great assemblies in this universe. Furthermore, when I had descended from the palace of Lord Indra to the bodhi tree in this world of Jambudvipa, I uttered the precepts which are always recited when one first gives rise to the mind [which aspires for enlightenment]. This I did for the benefit of all worldly beings among the living creatures of this world. [The precepts themselves] arose out of the fundamental words of Dharma of Rocana Buddha, my original being. Such precepts are called the "diamonds of brilliant light". They are the source of all Buddhas; the root of all bodhisattvas; and the original Buddha-nature itself.

Because all sentient beings are endowed with the Buddha-nature, they possess form, thought and consciousness. Thought and consciousness are thus contained within the ethical principle of the Buddha-nature. And because the basic cause [i.e. the Buddha-nature] is always present [in beings], the Dharma-body is likewise always there. As a result of these conditions, the ten major ethical precepts come into being. All sentient beings throughout the three worlds should respectfully observe these Dharma precepts. Once they have been received, they should be carefully guarded.

For the benefit of those gathered here, I will now once again expound the chapter concerning the "inexhaustible treasury of precepts". These are the precepts upon which all sentient beings should depend. Their fundamental nature is completely pure.

> Now, I, Rocana Buddha, am seated on a lotus throne
> Surrounded by one thousand flowers on each of which are found
> A thousand Shakyamunis and one hundred million worlds.
> And in each of these worlds appears a Shakyamuni.
> At exactly the same time each one of them sits beneath the bodhi tree
>   And realizes awakening.
> Likewise, Rocana Buddha is the fundamental body of these hundred thousand
>   million Buddhas.
> Every one of these hundred thousand million Shakyamuni Buddhas
>   is guiding numberless sentient beings.

Upon reaching the abode of Rocana they all come to perceive the exquisite
    Dharma-precepts.
Thus the door of ambrosia [i.e. immortality] opens wide.
Subsequently all the forms of Shakyamuni Buddha
Return to their own worlds and, seated again beneath the bodhi tree,
Proceed to recite in order the ten major and the forty-eight minor precepts
Expounded by [Rocana Buddha,] their original teacher.
These precepts are as brilliant as the sun and the moon and glow like pearls.
Because of them innumerable bodhisattvas have been able to realize
    Complete and perfect awakening.
In a similar way I am now going to recite
These precepts which were originally delivered by Rocana Buddha.
Likewise, you bodhisattvas who are new to the path must respectfully
    Observe them.
And, having kept them purely, transmit them to all sentient beings.

These precepts which you should attentively listen to and memorize
Are the rules of the Buddhadharma called the *Pratimoksha*.
All of you gathered here should have complete faith in them.
In the future you will all become Buddhas just as I have become a Buddha.
Just having faith in this path is sufficient
For you to be completely in possession of the precepts even now.
All those who have a mind should receive these precepts without fail.
For once the Buddha precepts have been received,
Buddhahood is sure to be reached. Then one becomes a true Buddha
Since one's state can no longer be distinguished from great awakening.
So, all of you gathered here,
Listen to my Dharma precepts with all of your respect and attention.

After Shakyamuni Buddha had realized the unsurpassable perfect
awakening beneath the bodhi tree, he formulated, for the first
time, the *Pratimoksha* of the bodhisattvas. This entails being
devoted[1] to the Three Jewels, one's teachers and one's parents. It is
the Dharma of being devoted[1a] to the true way. Such devotion[1b] is
called both *sila* [ethics, precepts] and *vinaya* [discipline, control].

The Buddha then emitted from his mouth an immeasurably brilliant light. As this light shone forth, the millions of assemblies, the
multitude of bodhisattvas, the celestials of the eighteen realms of
Brahma and the lords of the six realms of desire, as well as the kings
of the sixteen countries, all joined their palms together and listened
to the Mahayana precepts which the Buddha proceeded to recite.

The Buddha then said to the bodhisattvas, "Every fifteen days I will recite the Dharma precepts of the numerous Buddhas. Likewise those bodhisattvas who have resolved to attain enlightenment as well as the bodhisattvas of the ten Initial Stages [and] the bodhisattvas of the ten Developmental Stages. The bodhisattvas of the ten Diamond Stages of firmness, and the bodhisattvas of the ten Grounds should also recite them. Thereupon the light of the precepts will be emitted from their mouths. Such light is not something which appears fortuitously without a cause. Neither is it something blue, yellow, red, white or black in colour; nor is it physical or mental; nor is it something either existent or non-existent; nor does it pertain to the law of cause and effect. In reality it is the source of all the Buddhas. It is what originally establishes the path of the bodhisattvas. It is the source of the assembly of the Buddha's sons. Therefore, all sons of the Buddha should receive and keep these precepts. They should recite them and learn them well.

"Disciples of the Buddha, listen carefully! Whoever receives these precepts, be they kings, princes, government officials, ministers of state, bhikshus, bhikshunis, celestials of the eighteen realms of Brahma, lords of the six realms of desire, ordinary people, eunuchs, sensuous men or women, servants, one of the eight kinds of demons, guardian spirits, animals, spirits which have assumed human form, as long as they can understand the words of the teacher of Dharma, will be called 'immaculate'."

The Buddha then said to his many disciples, "There are ten major *Pratimoksha*. If someone who has received the bodhisattva precepts fails to recite or memorize them, he can be called neither a bodhisattva nor a disciple of the Buddha. It is for this reason that I too am reciting them. Numerous bodhisattvas have learnt them in the past, are learning them now and will learn them in the future. Once the basic forms of the *Pratimoksha* have been outlined, then learn them well and keep them carefully."

Having said this, the Buddha then proceeded to enumerate them in the following way.

III

Ten Major Precepts &
Forty-Eight Secondary Precepts

1. Refrain from taking life

A disciple of the Buddha must refrain from taking life either by performing the act of killing himself, by causing someone else to do it, by doing it in a roundabout way, by "praising" death [i.e. encouraging someone to take his own life], or by the use of spells and mantras. One must never intentionally kill a living creature by creating the causes or conditions for death, by developing a means of taking life, or by engaging in the actual deed of killing. It is the duty of a bodhisattva to be always compassionate and devoted[1c] towards others and to lead them all to liberation by whatever means possible. If, on the contrary, a bodhisattva were to take a great deal of pleasure in killing others, this would be an extremely serious transgression for him.

2. Refrain from taking what is not given

A disciple of the Buddha must refrain from taking what is not given either by performing the act of stealing himself, by causing someone else to do it, by doing it in a roundabout way, or by the use of spells and mantras. One must never create the causes and conditions for stealing to take place, devise a means for stealing, or engage in the very act of stealing. One must never intentionally steal anything, not even a single needle or a tiny plant, no matter whether it belongs to another person, to a spirit, or has previously been stolen by a thief. It is the duty of a bodhisattva to make others joyful and happy by always presenting a state of mind which conforms to Buddha-nature. If, on the contrary, a bodhisattva were to steal the property of others, this would be an extremely serious transgression for him.

3. Refrain from improper sexual behaviour

A disciple of the Buddha must refrain from sexual misconduct either by committing an improper act himself, by causing someone else to engage in such acts, or by indulging in sexual relations indiscriminately with any creature of the opposite sex. He must never create the causes and conditions for sexual misconduct to occur, devise means whereby it can be engaged in, or perform the actual deeds himself. He must never intentionally engage in sexual relations with animals, celestials or spirits of the opposite sex. He must never perform perverted or indecent sexual acts. It is the duty of a bodhisattva always to present a state of mind which conforms to the Buddha-nature and to lead others to liberation by teaching them the pure Dharma. If, on the contrary, a bodhisattva were to entertain lustful thoughts indiscriminately with regard to living creatures, such that he failed even to distinguish between animals on the one hand, and his mother, daughters, sisters and six forms of family relation on the other, and were then to engage in improper sexual behaviour, this would cause compassion to disappear and would be an extremely serious transgression for him.

4. Refrain from telling lies

A disciple of the Buddha must refrain from telling lies either by doing so himself, by causing someone else to do so, or by doing so in a roundabout way. He must never create the causes and conditions for telling lies, devise a means for doing so, or actually tell them himself. He must never convey the impression that he saw something that he did not see, or did not see something that he did see, either by physical gestures or by his mental intention. It is the duty of a bodhisattva to maintain correct views and speak truthfully himself as well as to encourage others to behave likewise. Thus it is an extremely serious transgression for a bodhisattva to cause other beings to harbour false views, speak false words, or commit incorrect actions.

5. Refrain from selling alcohol

A disciple of the Buddha must refrain from selling alcohol himself or causing someone else to sell it. He must never create the causes and conditions for selling any kind of alcohol, devise a means of selling it, or actually sell it himself. Alcohol itself is a conditional factor in the committing of evil deeds. It is the duty of a bodhisattva to cultivate brilliant wisdom in the minds of living beings. If, on the contrary, he were to lead them into confusion, this would be an extremely serious transgression for him.

6. Refrain from discussing the faults of the fourfold assembly

A disciple of the Buddha must refrain from discussing the faults of bodhisattvas who have left the householder's life, of those who remain in the householder's life, and of bhikshus and bhikshunis. He must neither speak such words himself nor cause others to say them. He must never create the causes and conditions for speaking ill of the fourfold assembly, devise a means for doing so, or actually engage in such speech himself. It is the duty of a bodhisattva to instruct compassionately those who hold heretical views as well as the unfortunate adherents of the Hinayana [literally "two vehicles" – *pratyeka* and *sravaka*]. Thus upon hearing such people talking of deeds which are not in accordance with the Dharma or which transgress the Buddhist ethical precepts and *vinaya*, he should cause these unfortunate beings to give rise to faith in the Mahayana. If instead a bodhisattva were to speak ill of the Buddhist community, this would be an extremely serious transgression for him.

7. Refrain from praising yourself and slandering others

A disciple of the Buddha must refrain from praising himself and slandering others either by doing so himself or by causing others to do so. He must never create the causes and conditions for praising himself and slandering others, devise a means of doing so, or actually engage in such deeds himself. It is the duty of a bodhisattva to take upon himself the slander directed towards others, to transfer whatever is unpleasant to himself, and to give whatever is good to others. But if, on the contrary, a bodhisattva were to make a display of his own virtue and wisdom and to conceal the virtues of others, thereby causing blame and slander to fall upon them [instead of him], this would be an extremely serious transgression for him.

8. Refrain from reviling others in order to spare oneself

A disciple of the Buddha must refrain from being miserly and must not encourage others to be so. He must never create the causes and conditions for miserliness, devise a means of being miserly, or harbour a miserly attitude himself. Should he be approached by a poor person begging for something, he should give whatever is requested. If, on the contrary, a bodhisattva, out of an angry or evil mind, does not give a beggar anything – not even a single penny, a needle or a tiny plant – or does not give someone in search of Dharma even a few words of advice, a single verse of teaching, or show him a little of the Buddha's way, but instead reviles him with harsh and evil words, this would be an extremely serious transgression for him.

9. Refrain from being angry. When someone comes to ask forgiveness, treat him well

A disciple of the Buddha must refrain from becoming angry himself and must not make others angry. He must never create the causes and conditions for becoming angry, devise a means of giving rise to anger or commit acts of anger himself. It is the duty of a bodhisattva to be always kind to others and never to quarrel with them. He should always present a compassionate and devout[1d] state of mind. If, on the contrary, a bodhisattva should abuse a living creature or vent his anger on an inanimate object and if – even though he may have resorted to beating them with his hand, a stick or a knife, and the person has politely begged forgiveness – his anger remains unappeased, this would be an extremely serious transgression for him.

10. Refrain from slandering the Three Jewels

A disciple of the Buddha must refrain from slandering the Three Jewels himself or causing someone else to slander them. He must never create the causes and conditions for such slander, devise a means of doing it, or engage in such an act himself. Should a bodhisattva hear even a single word against the Three Jewels uttered by an outsider [i.e. a non-Buddhist] or an evil person, he would feel as though his chest had been pierced by three hundred spears. So how could it be conceivable for him not to remain faithful and devout[1e] and to utter words of slander from his own mouth? Thus it is an extremely serious transgression for a bodhisattva to assist a heretically minded or evil person in slandering the Three Jewels.

These are the ten major precepts of the bodhisattva. They should be learnt without fail by all those who aspire to know them. Since one must not even transgress the tiniest particle of any one of these precepts, it should be unthinkable to consider transgressing all ten of them. If you transgress these precepts while in this present body, then you will be unable to produce the mind of awakening [*bodhicitta*]. Upon transgressing these precepts, kings, *chakravatins*, bhikshus or bhikshunis will all lose their position and status. Moreover, they will lose their position on the ten Initial Stages, the ten Developmental Stages, the ten Diamond Stages of firmness and the ten Grounds as well as the constant abiding wonderful fruit of the Buddha-nature. Having lost all of this they will then fall into the three unfortunate realms and for two or three aeons will be unable to hear even the name of the Three Jewels or of their parents. Hence not a single one of them must be transgressed. By having learnt them in the past, by learning them now and by continuing to learn them in the future, all bodhisattvas should certainly bring them to maturity and keep them with a respectful mind. The Buddha said to the bodhisattvas: "Now that the ten *Pratimoksha* have been spoken, the forty-eight secondary precepts will be expounded. They are explained clearly in the chapter 'Eighty Thousand Duties of a Bodhisattva'."[2]

THE FORTY-EIGHT SECONDARY PRECEPTS

1. Respect one's teachers and companions in the way

When a disciple of the Buddha attains the position of a king or a *chakravatin*, or when he is appointed to a government post, he must first receive the bodhisattva precepts. In this way the Buddha will be caused to rejoice and various spirits will protect his body. Once the precepts have been received, then upon meeting a venerable elder [*mahasthavira*], a venerable preceptor, a venerable teacher [*acarya*], a realized monk, a fellow practitioner, or one with the same knowledge and level of practice as himself, the bodhisattva must rise to greet them with a devout[f] mind. He must show them reverence and welcome them politely. But if, on the contrary, he does not rise to greet them, through arrogance, laziness, stupidity or anger, and fails to pay them any respect; or if he is unwilling to sell his own body,[3] his country, his sons and daughters, the seven kinds of jewel, or anything he may possess in order to provide them with food, thus failing to make an offering to them in accordance with the Dharma, then he breaks a secondary precept and commits a defiling offence.

2. Refrain from drinking alcohol

A disciple of the Buddha must refrain from drinking alcohol, because in doing so he will be made to commit unwholesome deeds. If one pours a glass of liquor and gives it to someone else to drink, the result will be that for five hundred lifetimes one will be born without hands. So how could one ever consider drinking it oneself? All people should endeavour to avoid drinking alcohol. And when one is trying to prevent all beings from drinking alcohol, how could one ever consider it permissible to drink it oneself? One must therefore refrain from drinking any kinds of intoxicating liquor. Anyone who intentionally drinks alcohol, or causes someone else to drink it, breaks a secondary precept and commits a defiling offence.

3. Refrain from eating meat[4]

A disciple of the Buddha must not eat any meat. It is forbidden to eat the flesh of any living creature. If he eats meat, he destroys great compassion and great kindness and the seed of the Buddha-nature. Upon seeing a person who eats meat, other beings will turn away from him. For these reasons a bodhisattva must not eat any meat. Eating meat is the source of innumerable evil deeds. To eat meat is therefore to break a secondary precept and commit a defiling offence.

4. Refrain from eating the five pungent vegetables[5]

A disciple of the Buddha must refrain from eating the five kinds of pungent and unwholesome vegetable, namely: garlic, leek, onion, rocambole and squill. To eat these intentionally in any form is to break a secondary precept and commit a defiling offence.

5. Cause someone who has transgressed the precepts to repent

Upon seeing someone transgress any of the five, eight or ten precepts, slander the Three Jewels, commit one of the seven heinous crimes, engage in an act which will cause them to be reborn in one of the eight difficult conditions, or break any kind of vow, a disciple of the Buddha must, without fail, cause him to repent what he has done. It is not permissible for a bodhisattva who has not made a certain person repent to then enjoy the benefit of receiving offerings together with that person. Moreover, if he is in the company of such a person at the time of the ceremony of purification, while the precepts are being recited to the gathered assembly [or on any other occasion], and he fails to make him repent by pointing out his misdeeds to him, then he breaks a secondary precept and commits a defiling offence.

6. Make offerings to teachers and request the Dharma

Upon meeting a teacher of the Mahayana, a fellow student of the Mahayana, or someone with the same knowledge and level of practice as himself approaching a temple or a village after having walked for a hundred or a thousand *li*, a disciple of the Buddha must rise to greet him, pay him respects and provide him with food. Three times every day he should prepare for and offer to such persons various fine foods worth four ounces of gold. Moreover, he should provide any Dharma teacher with a wooden bed, medicines, or whatever else he may need. In the morning, at noon and in the evening, he should request instructions on the Dharma. He must make the request with a reverent mind without getting angry or becoming troublesome. In order to receive such instruction, he should be prepared to forget about his own body and put all his efforts into seeking the Dharma. Not to act in this way is to break a secondary precept and commit a defiling offence.

7. Always attend a lecture on Dharma whenever it is held

If the Buddhadharma is being taught in a large mansion, or if the sutras, the *sila* and the *vinaya* are being expounded somewhere, then a disciple of the Buddha must go there to listen to what is being said. A bodhisattva at the beginning of his training should take the appropriate sutras or texts on *vinaya*, go to listen to the instructions of the Dharma teacher, and question him about what he has taught. Not to go and listen to the Buddhadharma when it is being expounded – be it in a temple, a forest or under a tree – and not to question the teacher is to break a secondary precept and commit a defiling offence.

8. Do not intentionally go against the Mahayana

For a disciple of the Buddha not to be well versed in the sutras and the *vinaya* of the everlasting Mahayana and to say that they are not the words of the Buddha; to follow the teaching contained in the sutras and the *vinaya* of the Hinayana; or to subscribe to the false opinions derived from the evil view of outsiders, constitutes breaking a secondary precept and committing a defiling offence.

9. Care well for those who are sick

Upon seeing someone who is afflicted with a disease, a disciple of the Buddha must care and provide for him as he would for the Buddha himself. First among the eight fields of blessing is that of nursing the sick. Whenever one's parents, teachers, disciples or anyone else is afflicted with a particular disease and their limbs or senses are impaired, then one should make an effort to help them recover. But should a bodhisattva – whether he be in a temple, a field, a forest, a path, or a mountain – fail to nurse and give assistance to someone who is sick, through thoughts of dislike and resentment, then he breaks a secondary precept and commits a defiling offence.

10. Do not keep and have ready for use any implements for killing

A disciple of the Buddha must not keep and have ready for use any implements which are needed for fighting, such as swords, clubs, bows, spears or hatchets. Nor must he keep or have ready for use any implement that can be employed for catching and killing animals, such as net, a lasso or a trap. When a bodhisattva should not take revenge [by killing] someone who has killed his parents, all the more so should he not kill any other living creatures. Therefore, he should never keep and have ready for use any implements that can be used for killing living beings. To do so intentionally results in breaking a secondary precept and committing a defiling offence.

With an attitude of respect, one should learn the above ten precepts well, adhere to them and uphold them. They are explained clearly in the chapter "Six Perfections".[6]

11. Do not become the military envoy of a country

A disciple of the Buddha must not, out of evil motivation, seeking profit and gain for himself, become a military envoy, conduct meetings [between enemies] on a battlefield, or incite people to fight a war in which many beings would be killed. When a bodhisattva should not even set foot in an army camp, how could he engage in rebellious acts and seditious acts which would be harmful to the nation? Deliberately to do such work is to break a secondary precept and commit a defiling offence.

12. Refrain from doing business with evil intent

A disciple of the Buddha must not buy or sell [free] citizens, slaves, or any of the six kinds of [domestic] animal. He must not sell a coffin, planks to make a coffin or anything which can be used to contain a corpse. And if a bodhisattva should not do any of these things himself, how could he ever encourage others to do them? To trade in these things intentionally or make others do so results in breaking a secondary precept and committing a defiling offence.

13. Refrain from slandering others

A disciple of the Buddha must never, with evil intent, baselessly slander good citizens, virtuous people, teachers of the Dharma, monks, kings by saying that they have committed such deeds as the seven heinous crimes or the ten major transgressions. He should always nurture a devoted[18] and compassionate attitude towards his parents, brothers and sisters and all the other six kinds of family relative. If, on the contrary, he intentionally causes them suffering and makes them go to an undesirable place, he would break a secondary precept and commit a defiling offence.

14. Do not light destructive fires

A son of the Buddha must not, with evil intent, set fire to mountains, plains, meadows from the fourth to the ninth month, other people's houses, cities, temples, cultivated fields, forests, goods belonging to a spirit, or any public property. He must not intentionally burn any living creatures. To light such fires deliberately is to break a secondary precept and commit a defiling offence.

15. Refrain from teaching the incorrect doctrines of others

A son of the Buddha must always uphold the sutras and the *vinaya* of the Mahayana and teach them [to all] without distinguishing between Buddhists and outsiders, evil people and his relatives and friends. Making people see the meaning and principles contained in such words will cause them to give rise to the mind of enlightenment, as well as progress through the ten Initial minds, the ten Developmental minds, the ten Diamond minds of firmness. One should then make people aware of the order and individual functions of the Dharma revealed in these various states of mind. But, if on the contrary, a bodhisattva were to teach perversely, with evil and hateful thoughts, the sutras and the *vinaya* of the Hinayana or the incorrect views and doctrines of the outsiders, this would be breaking a secondary precept and committing a defiling offence.

16. Teach correctly and do not be greedy for offerings

A son of the Buddha must first, with good intention, learn well the rules of dignified conduct, the sutras and the *vinaya* of the Mahayana and then clearly understand their meaning. If another bodhisattva, who has only recently raised the mind of enlightenment, should come from a hundred or a thousand *li* away in order to study the sutras and the *vinaya* of the Mahayana, then [he first should] instruct him well in the ascetic practices. Make it clear that if one does not burn one's body, arms and fingers as an offering to the Buddha, then one is not a bodhisattva who has left home and truly raised the mind of awakening. One should willingly give one's body,[3a] one's flesh, one's hand and feet to be eaten by starving tigers, wolves, lions and even hungry ghosts. [The bodhisattva] should then cause the mind of the other person to open up and understand the meaning of the true Dharma as he explains it to him in the correct order. If, on the contrary, for the sake of gain and offerings, a bodhisattva were not to give an answer when he should have given an answer, or were to teach the sutras and the *vinaya* in the wrong way, thereby causing their meaning to seem the opposite of what it is and the Three Jewels to be slandered, this would be to break a secondary precept and commit a defiling offence.

17. Do not beg for and try to obtain things by relying upon the authorities

A disciple of the Buddha must not extort money or goods or seek any other kind of gain through relying upon the power of a king, a prince, a minister of state or government official with whom he is closely acquainted. To do such things by beating others or threatening them with violence is known as "seeking gain through evil means". Excessively to seek such gain or to encourage someone else to do this is to discard a compassionate and devoted[1h] mind; one is breaking a secondary precept and committing a defiling offence.

18. Do not become a teacher while knowing nothing of what you are teaching

A disciple of the Buddha must learn well the twelve categories of sutra and, if he is a reciter of the bodhisattva precepts, must familiarize himself with them six times a day at the prescribed times. He must have a good understanding of their meaning as well as the principles concerning the nature of the Buddha. But should a bodhisattva who knows not even a single word from a sutra or a single line from a verse of teaching, and who has no knowledge of the reasons why the precepts or the discipline came about, still pretend to know something, then he would only be deceiving himself and others. Thus to take the role of a teacher or become an instructor of the precepts while knowing nothing about the Dharma is to break a secondary precept and commit a defiling offence.

19. Refrain from divisive speech

When a disciple of the Buddha sees a bhikshu who acts in accordance with the precepts carrying an incense burner or performing the activities of a bodhisattva, he must not maliciously give rise to quarrels and disputes. To commit such evil deeds as slandering virtuous people is to break a secondary precept and commit a defiling offence.

20. Save the lives of living creatures and set loose those about to be killed

Out of his compassion a disciple of the Buddha must set free living creatures. Since all male creatures have at one time been one's father, they should all be regarded as one's father. And since all female creatures have at one time been one's mother, they should be regarded as one's mother. In each life they have been those who have given birth to one. All sentient beings throughout the six realms can therefore be considered one's father and mother. Thus to catch and eat any living creatures is surely equivalent to killing one's own parents and eating one's old body because the four great elements of earth, water, fire and air have been the original components of one's own body. For these reasons, one should always practise setting free all living creatures. Considering the eternally abiding Dharma of receiving life at each rebirth, one should also teach others to free living creatures.

When one sees someone trying to kill an animal, one should use all means possible to save the animal from such misfortune. Furthermore, one must also save living beings by always telling them of the bodhisattva precepts and instructing them in their meaning. On the days when a memorial service is held for one's parents or siblings, one must invite a Dharma teacher to read the bodhisattva precepts, the sutras or the *vinayas*, and to pray for the future happiness of the departed ones in order that they may encounter the Buddha and take birth in the human and celestial realms. Failure to do any of the things stated above results in breaking a secondary precept and committing a defiling offence.

With an attitude of respect, one should learn the above ten precepts well, adhere to them and uphold them. The characteristics of the precepts have been explained clearly one by one in the chapter "Extinguishing Wrongdoings".[6a]

21. Refrain from anger; do not strike others; and do not take revenge

A disciple of the Buddha must not repay anger with anger or blows with blows. Even if someone were to kill his parents, his siblings, any of the six kinds of his close relatives, or the king, he must refrain from taking revenge. To take revenge on someone who has killed by killing him is not in accordance with the principle of devotion.[1i] When one should daily avoid committing any misdeeds of body, speech and mind against one's servant by beating and scolding them, because this would be committing immeasurable crimes with the mouth, then how could one ever commit any of the seven heinous crimes? For a bodhisattva who has left the householder's life,[7] to abandon a compassionate mind and to take revenge intentionally even against an enemy of one of the six kinds of his close relatives is to break a secondary precept and commit a defiling offence.

22. Relinquishing pride, request the Dharma

When a disciple of the Buddha first leaves the householder's life and still has little understanding, he must not feel averse to learning the sutras or the *vinaya* from a Dharma teacher who has already studied them, because he believes his own wisdom to be naturally bright, that he is of a higher social standing, is more advanced in years, comes from a superior lineage, has greater blessings, or owns more property or riches. Even though a teacher of the Dharma may be young in years, come from an insignificant lineage, be poor, have coarse features, or even have impaired senses, if he truly practises morality and is well versed in the sutras and *vinaya*, then a bodhisattva who is starting his training should seek him out without paying any attention to such things as his lineage, and proceed to learn the supreme truth from him. Not to do so results in breaking a secondary precept and committing a defiling offence.

23. Do not be biased in what you teach because of pride

If, with a wholesome mind, a disciple of the Buddha wishes to receive the bodhisattva precepts at a time after the Buddha's entrance into Nirvana, he can make a sincere vow before an image of a Buddha or a bodhisattva. If, after having taken the precepts and repented to the Buddhas and bodhisattvas for seven days, he sees certain auspicious signs, then he can be sure that the precepts have been secured. However, if auspicious signs are not seen, he must continue to do acts of repentance for fourteen or twenty-one days or even for a year until such signs appear. Once the auspicious signs are beheld, then he can take the precepts before an image of a Buddha or a bodhisattva. As long as these auspicious signs do not appear, then no matter how much he makes a vow before images of Buddhas and bodhisattvas, the precepts cannot be received.

If the precepts are taken from a Dharma teacher who has previously received them himself, then there is no need for auspicious signs to appear. In such a case the appearance of these signs is unnecessary because the precepts will actually have been transmitted through a succession of Dharma teachers. Therefore, to take the precepts from a qualified Dharma teacher ensures their being secured. Moreover they are secured because one has given rise to a mind which esteems them highly. But if there is no Dharma teacher within a thousand *li* and one has to take the precepts before an image of the Buddha or a bodhisattva, then it is necessary to see auspicious signs.

If, because of disdain, dislike or pride, a Dharma teacher who relies upon a thorough knowledge of the sutras, the *vinaya* and the Dharma of the Mahayana, but also has a close acquaintance with a king, a prince or a government official, does not give good and detailed instructions about the sutras and the *vinaya* to a bodhisattva who, just starting his training, has asked him about such things, then he breaks a secondary precept and commits a defiling offence.

24. Refrain from not learning the Dharma well

There are some disciples of the Buddha who, despite the fact that there exist the sutras, the *vinaya* and the Dharma of the Mahayana as well as correct views, the true nature and the true Dharma-body of the Buddha, do not diligently study these things and thus cast aside the most precious jewels in the world. Instead they study the *Abhidharma* commentaries of the Hinayana, doctrines created out of the wrong views of the outsiders, worldly knowledge, and other diverse written materials. To study such material crushes the Buddha-nature. Since it is a causal condition which obstructs the Way, such people are not following the path of the bodhisattvas. Thus one breaks a secondary precept and commits a defiling offence when deliberately pursuing such study.

25. Guide the community well and maintain it in harmony

At the time after the Nirvana of the Buddha, if a disciple of the Buddha has become a vinaya preceptor or a Dharma master, the abbot of a monastery, a preacher, a meditation master, or a guest master, he must satisfactorily settle any disputes [within the community] with a compassionate attitude. Moreover, he must safeguard the possessions of the Three Jewels and never use them carelessly as he would his own possessions. Thus to create disorder in the community and provoke quarrels and disputes, or to use the possessions of the Three Jewels carelessly, is to break a secondary precept and commit a defiling offence.

26. Do not accept offerings for yourself alone

If a disciple of the Buddha living in a particular temple, a house, a city, a temple built by the king, or a place where a three-month retreat is being held, or in quarters used by a great assembly, sees bhikshus or bodhisattvas enter, he and any others already in that place must rise to greet the guests and finally see them off well. They must provide the guests with whatever they need: food and drink, lodging, bedding, wooden beds, cushions and so forth. If they have nothing to give them, then they should be willing to supply them with all the essentials even if it means selling their own body[3b] or that of their son or daughter, or cutting off their flesh and selling it. Furthermore, if a layperson extends an invitation to the assembly, the monks who are guests should receive a share of the offerings. The abbot must make sure that they receive them in accordance with the proper order. If only those who are already living in a particular place receive the offerings and prevent the guests from partaking of them, the abbot will accumulate innumerable evils. He should be considered as no different from an animal. He is not a true monk, or a disciple of the Buddha. To commit such a misdeed is to break a secondary precept and commit a defiling offence.

27. Do not accept an invitation for yourself alone

A disciple of the Buddha must never receive an invitation for himself alone, or enjoy the benefit of what is offered just by himself. The benefits of any offering belong to all the sangha of the ten directions. Thus to accept anything for oneself alone means to keep what rightfully belongs to the sangha of the ten directions. To take and use for oneself any article belonging to one of the eight fields of blessing – that is, a Buddha, an *arhat*, a *vinaya* preceptor, a Dharma teacher, the community of monks, one's father, one's mother or a sick person – results in breaking a secondary precept and committing a defiling offence.

28. Do not make individual invitations to the monks

When a disciple of the Buddha – whether he is a bodhisattva who has left the householder's life, a householder bodhisattva, or an ordinary layperson – intends to make a vow to invite the community of monks which is a field of blessing, then he should go to the monastery and tell the person in charge that he has made such a vow and intends to issue such an invitation. He should also inquire as to the proper means to go about his task. The person in charge should then reply that the monks must be invited in accordance with the proper order. For in this way he will receive noble monks from the ten directions. Even if someone were to invite separately five hundred *arhats* or monks who are bodhisattvas, this would not compare with inviting some ordinary monks in accordance with the proper order. To make individual invitations is the way of outsiders. For the seven Buddhas there exists no law for making individual invitations. To do so is not the way of true devotion.[1i] Thus deliberately to invite a monk individually is to break a secondary precept and commit a defiling offence.

29. Do not hold an unwholesome occupation

A disciple of the Buddha must not, with evil intention and for the sake of gain, engage in such occupations as selling physical charms of men and women, preparing food with his own hands, pounding grains with a pestle or grinding them in a mill, telling fortunes by looking at a person's physiognomy, interpreting dreams, predicting the sex of a child, making use of spells and magic, performing tricks in order to deceive others, domesticating hawks, preparing any kinds of dangerous drugs, or concocting poisons out of gold, silver or the venom of insects. Since such occupations are contrary to a mind of compassion and devotion,[1k] to engage in them deliberately results in breaking a secondary precept and committing a defiling offence.

30. Pay respect to the proper times and do not interfere with the laypeople[8]

A disciple of the Buddha should not, with evil intent, pretend to revere the Three Jewels while in fact reviling them; proclaim that things are empty but show a grasping at existence in his actions. Moreover one must not interfere with laypeople, so that men and women would assemble with the result that they commit improper sexual acts or form a variety of attachments and bonds. One must not influence them so that they kill living creatures[9] on the six specified fasting days and during the three special months of abstinence and care; or that they interrupt the period of abstinence, commit such acts as theft; or that they transgress any of the precepts. If a bodhisattva were to interfere in such a way it would result in breaking a secondary precept and committing a defiling offence.

With an attitude of respect one must learn the above ten precepts well, adhere to them and uphold them. They are explained clearly in the chapter "Restraints".[6b]

31. Pay ransom and rescue people from their difficulties

The Buddha said: "If, in this evil world which exists after the Nirvana of the Buddha, a disciple of the Buddha should see an outsider, a wicked person or a thief selling images of the Buddha, bodhisattvas, or their parents; trading in sutras or books of *vinaya*; or, having sold bhikshus, bhikshunis, bodhisattvas who have given rise to the mind of enlightenment, or men of the Way, making them become slaves or the servants of government officials, then with a compassionate mind he must use all possible skilful means in order to rescue them. Wherever one goes one must teach and transform others and try to raise the money needed to redeem the images of the Buddhas and bodhisattvas, and the sutras and *vinaya* texts, and to rescue the bhikshus, bhikshunis and bodhisattvas who have given rise to the mind of enlightenment. To fail to do so results in breaking a secondary precept and committing a defiling offence."

32. Do not cause harm to sentient beings

A disciple of the Buddha must not sell swords, clubs, or bows and arrows, nor shculd he use uneven balances or inaccurate weights and measures. One must not use one's influence with government offices to deprive others of their possessions; with harmful intent have others bound or shackled; undo the achievements of others; or breed domestic and wild cats, pigs, dogs and like creatures. To do such deeds deliberately is to break a secondary precept and commit a defiling offence.

33. Never even look at unwholesome things

A disciple of the Buddha must not, with evil intent, look at men or women who are quarrelling or fighting, at army encampments, at battles or at violent disputes among thieves. He should not watch or listen to music being played with shells, drums, harps, mandolins, flutes and similar instruments, nor should he watch dancing or listen to singing accompanied by a lute. One must not play such games as cards, *go*, chess, draughts, dice, ball sports, "stone throwing" and "pitching arrows into a pot". Moreover, one must not practise divination with mirrors made of claws, yarrow stalks, willow twigs, priest's bowls or skulls. One must never run errands for thieves. To perform any of these forbidden actions deliberately is to break a secondary precept and commit a defiling offence.

34. Never abandon the mind of enlightenment even for a moment

While walking, standing, lying down or sitting, during the six times of day and night, a disciple of the Buddha must familiarize himself with the precepts and keep them well. One must keep them as carefully as one would take care of a diamond, or hold on to a raft with which one hoped to cross the ocean, or as the bhikshu who was bound by grass would not uproot the grass to free himself.[10] One must always maintain faith in the Mahayana. Being aware that one is not yet a fully realized Buddha whereas those who are Buddhas are fully realized, one must give rise to the mind of enlightenment and must not forsake this attitude even for a moment. To give rise even for a moment to the attitude of the Hinayana or the outsiders results in a minor offence.

35. Make vows

A disciple of the Buddha must always make vows to be devoted to his parents[11] and his teachers. One should vow to meet good teachers and virtuous friends, to study with them always and receive instruction on the sutras and the *vinaya* texts of the Mahayana, as well as on the ten Initial Stages, the ten Developmental Stages, the ten Diamond Stages of firmness, and the ten Grounds, in order to develop a clear understanding and a practice which is in accordance with the Dharma, and to maintain firmly the precepts of the Buddha. Instead of allowing the precepts to disappear from one's mind for even an instant, one should prefer to lose one's body and one's life. For a bodhisattva not to make such vows results in breaking a secondary precept and committing a defiling offence.

36. Always make pledges

When a disciple of the Buddha has committed himself to the ten preceding great vows, he must maintain the precepts of the Buddha and make the following pledges:[3c]

I would rather this body be cast into a roaring fire, a deep pit, or onto a mountain of swords than ever to vilify the sutras or the precepts of the Buddhas of the three periods by indulging in unchaste acts with the various beings of the opposite sex. I would rather this body be wrapped around a thousand times by a red-hot iron net than, having transgressed the precepts with my body, ever be clothed with garments offered by sincere laypeople. I would rather eat with this mouth balls of red-hot iron and fire for a hundred thousand aeons than, having transgressed the precepts in my speech, ever eat any food or drinks offered by sincere laypeople. I would rather lay this body down on a sheet of red-hot iron surrounded by a wall of blazing fire than, having transgressed the precepts, ever be seated on beds or cushions offered by sincere laypeople.

I would rather this body experience the suffering of being pierced by three hundred spears for one or two aeons than, having transgressed the precepts with my body, ever receive any medicine from sincere laypeople. I would rather this body enter a boiling cauldron and spend a hundred thousand aeons there than, having transgressed the precepts with my body, ever make use of rooms, houses, forests, land and so forth offered by sincere laypeople. I would rather have this body broken apart with an iron hammer and entirely reduced to powder than, having transgressed the precepts with my body, ever receive respect and prostrations from sincere laypeople.

I would rather my two eyes be gouged out by a hundred or a thousand burning knives and spears than ever behold beautiful forms with a mind that has transgressed the precepts. I would rather my ears be pierced with a hundred thousand awls for one or two aeons than ever listen to pleasing sounds with a mind that has transgressed the precepts. I would rather my nose be severed by a hundred thousand knives than smell sweet fragrances with a mind that has transgressed the precepts. I would rather my tongue be lacerated with a hundred thousand knives than ever enjoy delicious foods with a mind that has transgressed the precepts. I would rather my body be hacked to pieces with a sharp axe than, having transgressed the precepts, enjoy what is pleasing to the touch. Moreover I vow that all sentient beings will become Buddhas. For a bodhisattva not to make such pledges is to break a secondary precept and commit a defiling offence.

37. Refrain from travelling in dangerous places

When a disciple of the Buddha is performing itinerant ascetic practices [dhuta] during the spring and autumn, when he is engaged in meditation during the summer and winter, or when he is partaking in a summer rains' retreat, he must always keep the following things with him: willow branches for cleaning the teeth, soap, the three essential monk's robes, a water container, a bowl, a mat, a staff, an incense burner, a filtering cloth, a towel, a knife, a flint, a pair of tweezers, bedding, sutras, vinaya texts and images of Buddhas and bodhisattvas. Whether a bodhisattva is performing specific acts of itinerant ascetic practices or whether he is simply travelling to places a hundred or a thousand li away, he must have in his possession these eighteen articles.

The times for performing itinerant ascetic practices are from the fifteenth of the first month to the fifteenth of the third month and from the fifteenth of the eighth month to the fifteenth of the tenth month.[11] During these two periods the eighteen articles should be considered as two wings of a bird that must never leave one's body.

Every fifteen days [while practising itinerant ascetic practices] the ceremony of purification [uposatha] must be conducted by the bodhisattvas who have recently given rise to the determination to realize enlightenment. On this occasion the ten major and the forty-eight minor vows must, without fail, be recited before images of the Buddhas and the bodhisattvas. On the occasion of the ceremony of purification a single person must recite the vows alone, no matter if he is the only person present or whether there are two, three, a hundred or a thousand people attending. The reciter must be seated in a high place and those listening in a lower place. Each one of them must wear the ceremonial robe [kasaya] of nine, seven, or five panels. The summer [rains] retreat too must be conducted in strict accordance with the Dharma.

While performing itinerant ascetic practices one must avoid travelling in dangerous places. Such places would include: an inhospitable country, a land governed by an evil king, a place where the ground is uneven, a place which is overgrown with vegetation, a place where there are lions, tigers and wolves, a place prone to floods, fires and gales, a remote road frequented by bandits or a place where there are snakes and other such dangers. Such places should be avoided not only while wandering around performing itinerant ascetic practices but also during the period of the summer [rains] retreat. To enter such places deliberately results in breaking a secondary precept and committing a defiling offence.

38. Do not disregard the order of "high" and "low"

A disciple of the Buddha must seat himself in the appropriate place as dictated by the Dharma. The first to have received the precepts should be seated in front, and the last to have received them should be seated behind. The order of the seating is not to be determined according to age. Instead, whenever bhikshus, bhikshunis, kings, princes, eunuchs, slaves and the like are gathered, then they should seat themselves according to the order in which they have received the precepts. Do not behave like the foolish outsiders who, taking no notice of either age or precedence, sit in no particular order. Moreover, do not follow the customs of the common soldiers or slaves. According to the doctrine of the Buddha, those who were first to receive the precepts should sit in the front and those who were last should sit at the rear. For a bodhisattva to disregard the correct order in which one should be seated is to break a secondary precept and commit a defiling offence.

39. Cultivate merit and wisdom

In addition to transforming all kinds of sentient beings through teaching them the Dharma, a disciple of the Buddha must arrange for temples to be built, mountains, forests and land to be prepared for housing religious facilities, stupas to be erected, and places to be organized where the summer and winter meditation retreats can be carried out and the Way cultivated.

For the sake of sentient beings, bodhisattvas should expound the sutras, the *vinaya* and the precepts of the Mahayana. They should read and explain these texts whenever disease is rampant; when a national crisis occurs; when thieves are about; on the death of their parents and siblings, *vinaya* preceptors and Dharma teachers, as well as on every seventh day from the third to the seventh week after their death. Likewise they should read and explain them when an assembly of monks is gathered to chant, on behalf of someone who has requested prayers to be said, when someone needs to be benefited in his daily life, when there is a fire or a flood, when a boat runs into a storm, or when someone is being troubled by the evil spirits of rivers, lakes or oceans.

Moreover, they should be read and explained while one is suffering the negative consequences of one's evil deeds, when one is born in the three unfortunate realms, when encountering the eight difficult conditions and the seven heinous crimes, and when one is bound with handcuffs, manacles or ropes, or is set in a pillory. Furthermore they should be read whenever greed, anger, ignorance and illness abound. Especially for someone who has recently become a bodhisattva, not to behave in this way results in breaking a secondary precept and committing a defiling offence.

With an attitude of respect, one should learn well the above nine precepts, adhere to them and uphold them. They are explained clearly in the chapter "Altar of Brahma".[6c]

40. Do not discriminate between those who come to receive the precepts

A disciple of the Buddha must not discriminate between those who have come to receive the precepts. Everyone must be able to receive them whether they be a king, prince, minister, government official, bhikshu, bhikshuni, layman, laywoman, a sensuous man or woman, a celestial in one of the eighteen realms of Brahma or a lord of the six celestial realms of desire, a person with no sexual organs, a hermaphrodite, eunuch, slave or any ghost or spirit.

They must be instructed that the ceremonial robe [*kasaya*] they wear is to be dyed with a combination of colours. In accordance with the Dharma one must remove the original colour of the cloth by dyeing the material with a mixture of blue, yellow, red, black and purple dyes. All clothing as well as bedding must be dyed with the same blend and have the same neutral tones. A bhikshu's clothes must be different from clothing worn by the laypeople of his country.

When someone wishes to receive the precepts, the Dharma teacher must ask him whether, in his present body, he has committed any of the seven heinous crimes. Someone who has committed one of the seven heinous crimes cannot be instructed in the bodhisattva precepts by a Dharma teacher. The seven heinous crimes are (1) to shed a Buddha's blood, (2) to kill one's father, (3) to kill one's mother, (4) to kill a preceptor [upadhyaya], (5) to kill a Dharma teacher [acarya], (6) to disrupt the harmony of the monastic community, and (7) to kill an arhat. Although those who have committed any of these seven heinous crimes cannot receive the precepts in their present body, all others are permitted to receive them.

A person who has renounced the householder's life must not bow to the king, his parents, or any of the six kinds of close relatives, nor to spirits.

If, out of malice, a Dharma teacher does not give the precepts, which all sentient beings are entitled to receive, to a person who is capable of understanding his words and has come to receive them from him after walking a hundred or a thousand li, then he breaks a secondary precept and commits a defiling offence.

41. Do not become a Dharma teacher for the sake of gain

When a disciple of the Buddha teaches and transforms others in order to make them develop faith, and if as a bodhisattva he can serve as a Dharma teacher capable of instructing people in the precepts, then, when he sees someone who wishes to receive the precepts, he must counsel him to invite two masters: a vinaya preceptor and a Dharma teacher. These two preceptors must ask the person who intends to receive the precepts whether or not he has committed any of the seven heinous crimes which would make him incapable of receiving them. A person who has committed any of these crimes must not be instructed in the precepts. But the teachers must instruct those who have not committed them.

A person who transgresses any of the ten major precepts should be taught to make repentance before images of the Buddha and bodhisattvas. He or she must recite the ten major and forty-eight minor precepts during the six periods of the day and night, pay respect with great devotion[1m] to the Buddhas of the three worlds and finally behold certain auspicious signs. If such signs are not beheld after seven, fourteen, twenty-one days or even a year, one must still continue with one's repentance until they do appear. An auspicious sign would be, for example, to have one's head touched by the Buddha or the appearance of a brilliant light, flowers or other extraordinary things. When such signs appear, one can be certain that one's offence has been eradicated. But if such signs do not appear, then repentance will have been of no use. In this case the person will be unable to receive the precepts again in his present body. But he has increased his merits to receive them [in a future life].

Upon transgressing one of the forty-eight minor precepts, the offence can be eradicated simply by making repentance [to a preceptor]. [However, no amount of repentance is able to eradicate the offence of committing] one of the seven heinous crimes which makes one completely unable to receive the precepts. A Dharma teacher who is responsible for giving instructions in the precepts should know such laws as these well. Moreover, a teacher should have a clear knowledge of what is minor and what is serious, of whether something is right or wrong in terms of the sutras and the *vinaya* of the Mahayana. He should know what is the fundamentally true principle, the nature of "the potential formed through practice", the "developmental" nature, the nature of "the naturally present potential", the "indestructible" nature, the nature endowed with the potential for Buddhahood, and the nature in accordance with the true Dharma. Furthermore, he must understand the various methods of contemplation which are derived from these principles and natures as well as the ten modes of meditation and all other such means of cultivating the mind. But if he remains ignorant of the true meaning of any of these doctrines, or if he is motivated solely by greed for material gain and renown, or if he just pretends to know the sutras and the *vinaya* in order to amass disciples, thus deceiving both himself and others for the sake of receiving offerings, for him then to give the precepts deliberately results in breaking a secondary precept and committing a defiling offence.

42. Do not expound the precepts to evil people

For the sake of obtaining personal benefits, a disciple of the Buddha must not, except in the case of a king of a country [whose role it is to protect the Dharma], expound the great precepts which have been taught by the thousand Buddhas to people who have not received them, to outsiders or evil people or anyone who holds erroneous views. Since such evil people do not receive the precepts of the Buddha, they are fit only to be called animals. In every world in which they are born they are unable to behold the Three Jewels. It is because they are as mindless as trees and stones that they are regarded as outsiders and as people with erroneous views. They are really no different from pieces of wood. Therefore, it is breaking a secondary precept and committing a defiling offence for a bodhisattva to expound the precepts taught by the seven Buddhas in the presence of such people.

43. Do not even think of transgressing the precepts

Once a disciple of the Buddha has left the householder's life with faithful intent and received the true precepts of the Buddha, then should he deliberately give rise to thoughts of transgressing his precepts, he will become unworthy to receive the offerings of any laypeople, to wander in the territory of a king and even to drink the water of that country. The five thousand great spirits will always stand in the way of such a person and call him a great thief. Upon entering a house in the countryside or a residence in a town or any other place they will sweep away all traces of him. People will scold him and call him a Buddhist thief. All kinds of sentient beings will not even set their eyes upon someone who has transgressed the precepts. Therefore, such people cannot be considered to be different from animals or pieces of wood. For a bodhisattva to transgress the true precepts deliberately results in breaking a secondary precept and committing a defiling offence.

44. Make offerings to the sutras and the *vinaya*

With a constant mind a disciple of the Buddha must always receive, keep, read and recite the sutras and the *vinaya* of the Mahayana. He must be willing to write down the precepts of the Buddha by peeling off his skin[3d] and using it as paper, draining his blood and using it as ink, extracting his marrow and using it as liquid for the ink-stone, and splitting his bones and using them as brushes. He should preserve the precepts by inscribing them on tree-bark, paper, silk, white fabric and bamboo. He should enclose the sutras and the *vinaya* texts in bags and boxes which have been made out of the seven jewels, sweet-smelling substances, flowers and all kind of precious materials. For a bodhisattva not to make such an offering in accordance with the Dharma results in breaking a secondary precept and committing a defiling offence.

45. Always teach sentient beings

A disciple of the Buddha should always produce a compassionate mind when he enters a house in the countryside or in a town and sees any sentient beings. He should say to them: "You, sentient beings, should take refuge in the Three Jewels and receive the ten major precepts." When he sees such animals as cows, horses, pigs, sheep and the like, he should think within himself and tell them with his mouth:[12] "You were born as animals, give rise to the mind of enlightenment." Wherever a bodhisattva travels – in mountains, forests, river valleys or fields – he must encourage all beings he meets to give rise to the mind of enlightenment. Failure to make the resolve to teach and transform sentient beings results in breaking a secondary precept and committing a defiling offence.

46. Teach the Dharma in accordance with the Dharma

A disciple of the Buddha must always transform people though teaching them with a mind of great compassion. When expounding the Dharma in the house of a layperson, to nobility or to a crowd, do not do so while standing among people. The Dharma must be taught while seated on a high seat placed before the assembled laity. A bhikshu who is also a Dharma teacher must never expound the Dharma to the fourfold assembly while standing on the ground among them. When the time comes to teach the Dharma, the Dharma master must sit on a raised seat and make sure there is an offering of incense and flowers. The members of the fourfold assembly should sit in a lower place and listen to the teachings of their preceptor with the same devotion[1n] as they would show to their parents and the same attention a brahmin would give to his sacrificial fire. To expound the Dharma in a manner which is not in accordance with the Dharma results in breaking a secondary precept and committing a defiling offence.

47. Do not establish regulations on the basis of an erroneous law

Once a disciple of the Buddha – be he a king, a prince, a government official or a member of the fourfold assembly – has received the precepts with a sincere and faithful mind, he must never claim to be a superior being and, having convinced himself of this, then proceed to destroy the Buddhadharma and the precepts by creating erroneous laws and taking disciplinary actions to limit the activities of the fourfold assembly. Thus he must never obstruct someone from leaving the householder's life in order to cultivate the way. Neither must he ever prevent the making of images of the Buddha or the construction of stupas, or hinder the copying of sutras and *vinayas*. He must not maintain an administration which places regulations and restrictions on the activities of the sangha. Nor must he spread such customs as having bodhisattvas who are monks stand on the ground while laypeople are seated in a high place or treat the monks like common soldiers or slaves serving their master. When a bodhisattva is worthy of receiving the offerings of all people, how could he ever become the servant of a government official? Thus if a king or a government official has received the precepts of the Buddha with a wholesome mind, he must never commit any offence which leads to the destruction of the Three Jewels. To destroy the Buddhadharma deliberately is to break a secondary precept and commit a defiling offence.

48. Do not destroy the Dharma

If a disciple of the Buddha who has left the householder's life with a wholesome mind should, while expounding the precepts of the Buddha in the presence of a king or government officials, for the sake of gain and renown, wilfully cause the arrest and incarceration of someone who has received the bhikshu, bhikshuni or bodhisattva precepts, this would be following the customs one finds in prisons and among common soldiers or slaves. Such a person would be similar to a worm which has been born in the body of a lion and is eating its flesh. A disciple of the Buddha who acts in this way destroys the Buddhadharma himself. Just as any other kind of worm is incapable of devouring the lion, so is an outsider or even the army of *Mara* incapable of destroying the Buddhadharma.

Once one has received the precepts of the Buddha, one must protect them and save them from destruction in the same way as one would cherish one's only son or serve one's parents. On hearing outsiders or other evil people insult the precepts of the Buddha, a bodhisattva should feel as though three hundred spears have pierced his heart[3e] or as though his body is being cut down by a thousand swords or beaten by ten thousand cudgels. He should prefer to spend a hundred aeons in hell rather than ever hear a single evil word which slanders the precepts of the Buddha. All the more so, how could a bodhisattva ever break one of the precepts himself or encourage others to do so thereby creating the causes and conditions for the destruction of the Buddhadharma? Moreover this would be a lack of devotion.[10] To do such things deliberately results in breaking a secondary precept and committing a defiling offence.

With an attitude of respect one should learn the above nine precepts well, adhere to them and uphold them.

Every disciple of the Buddha should receive and uphold these forty-eight minor precepts. The bodhisattvas of the past have recited them; the bodhisattvas of the present are reciting them; and the bodhisattvas of the future will recite them.

IV

Conclusion

Disciples of the Buddha, listen carefully! The Buddhas of the three worlds have recited the ten major and the forty-eight secondary precepts in the past, are reciting them in the present and will recite them in the future. Likewise I too have recited them now. So, all of you gathered here – kings, princes, government officials, bhikshus, bhikshunis, men and women of good faith – you who have received the bodhisattva precepts should [continue to] receive and uphold these precepts in which the Buddha-nature always resides. You should read them, recite them, expound them, explain them, write them down with a brush, and thus spread them to the sentient beings throughout the three worlds ensuring that their transformation be uninterrupted. In doing so they will be assured of meeting the thousand Buddhas and receiving their blessings and support. Wherever you are born you will be saved from falling into the three unfortunate realms or encountering the eight difficult conditions and will always find yourselves in the human or celestial realms.

Beneath the bodhi tree, I have now given a general explanation of the precepts of the seven Buddhas. All of you here should learn these *Pratimoksha* with a constant mind, uphold them and joyfully act in accordance with them as they are found explained clearly in every detail in the middle of the exhortation section of the chapter "Signless Heavenly King".[6d]

Thereupon the learned assemblies in the three thousands worlds who had gathered to receive the bodhisattva precepts listened to the words of the Buddha and, with a respectful mind, received the

89

precepts, kept them and upheld them with joy. Just as was explained above, Shakyamuni Buddha gave a complete exposition of the Dharma of the ten inexhaustible precepts as is found in the chapter entitled the "Mind-Ground Dharma Discourse" which was originally spoken by Rocana Buddha in the world called the "Lotus Platform Treasury". At the same time one hundred thousand million Shakyamuni Buddhas [dwelling in their own abodes elsewhere] were likewise expounding these teachings. He delivered these Dharma discourses in ten stages, from the palace of Mahesvara to the place beneath the bodhi tree, in order to make the numerous bodhisattvas and the members of all the great assemblies keep, uphold, read and recite these [precepts]. And he explained them in the same way in which they have been explained here. In the worlds as numerous as particles of dust, the hundred thousand million worlds and the "Lotus Platform Treasury" world [all the other Buddhas did the same]. They also gave a complete exposition of the numberless treasuries of Dharma spoken by all Buddhas. These included the teachings on the treasury of mind, the treasury of earth, the treasury of ethical precepts, the treasury of infinite resolute actions and vows, the treasury of the cause and effect of the ever abiding Buddha-nature, and so forth. In this way all the sentient beings residing in these hundred thousand million worlds joyfully received, kept, upheld and acted in accordance with [the precepts]. When the form of the ground of mind unfolds wisely, it is like the discourse given in full in the middle of the chapter "Seven Actions of the Brilliant Flower Buddha King".[6e]

Those with a clear mind, strong patience and wisdom
Who are able to follow such Dharma as this
Will obtain five great benefits even before they become a Buddha.

First, they will be protected by the Buddhas of the ten directions who think of them compassionately.
Second, at death endowed with right view, they will be able to rejoice.
Third, they will be befriended by bodhisattvas wherever they are born.
Fourth, through the amassing of merit and virtue, they will accomplish the [aim of] the precepts and the perfections.
Fifth, in this and in the coming world they will abound with morality, happiness and wisdom.

90

Such people are true sons of the Buddhas.
The wise should reflect well on this.

Those who advocate an "I" and cling to phenomena
can never give rise to such Dharma.
Moreover in those who grasp at their attainment of extinction
there is no ground to plant the seed [of true awakening].
If you want to grow the sprout of awakening
and its great brightness to shine over the world,
Cultivate a quiet and contemplative state.

All the true forms of all Dharmas
Are neither born nor do they perish.
They never recur yet never cease.
They are neither the same nor different.
And likewise they neither come nor go.

With a constant mind, endowed with exhaustive skilful means,
Learn those tasks to be performed
By the bodhisattvas in their correct order.
Not to discriminate between there being no more to learn
and there being more to learn
Is called the Mahayana, the supreme path.
Therein disappears the evil of all trivial thoughts and words
And therefrom emerges the omniscience of all the Buddhas.

Therefore, all sons of the Buddha must quickly give rise to great courage,
Guard and protect the pure precepts
And the *vinaya* of the Buddha like a jewel.
For the bodhisattvas of the past have studied them;
The bodhisattvas of the present are studying them;
And the bodhisattvas of the future will also study them;
Such a task is praise by the holy sages
Since it is the place where the Buddha acts.
Having likewise expounded [these precepts] in the proper manner
I now give this infinite store of happiness and virtue
Back to all sentient beings.

May we thereby advance to all wisdoms.
May all those who are listening to these words of Dharma realize the Way of
the Buddha.

Here ends the Supplementary Volume to the Brahma's Net Sutra *spoken by the Buddha.*

V

Apology and Dedication

The apology to the Assembly which follows the recitation of the precepts

I [name] apologize with a respectful mind to the assembly. Now I have recited the precepts upon being requested to do so by the assembly of monks. However, as I have not diligently cultivated the three trainings [of ethics, concentration and wisdom], the words of the precepts must have been recited unevenly. Thus you have sat a long time and it must have been tiresome for you. Thereby have I caused you to suffer. Out of its compassion I hope that the assembly has been pleased [with my recitation].

The verse of dedication

Rare are the merits and virtues which proceed from reciting the precepts.
So may this limitless happiness now be dedicated to all living beings.
I truly hope that all creatures drowning [in the ocean of suffering]
May quickly be born in the land of Amitabha.
Homage to all the Buddhas of the three worlds
Throughout the ten directions!
Homage to all the great noble bodhisattvas!
Homage to the great perfection of wisdom.

Appendix
The Tibetan Bodhisattva Vows

Engaging bodhicitta

The vows taken as a sign of commitment to developing bodhicitta (awakening mind) are divided into two sections, consisting of eighteen root vows and forty-six branch vows.

The four conditions

Except for vows 9 and 18, four conditions are required to transgress the major vows completely.

Knowing but not caring that you are breaking a vow

Because you lack faith in karma you think that performing a negative action does not matter. Because of ignorance you may not think that the action is negative and you will act contrary to the vow. Recognizing that the action is negative makes the transgression incomplete.

Not abandoning all thought of repeating the action

If you do not regret the action and generate the wish to avoid it in the future, or if you even have the wish to repeat the action, then this contributes to a complete transgression. If you wish never to commit such an action again, then the transgression is incomplete.

Exulting or admiring yourself for having done the action

For example, if you break the first vow and then think, "How good it was that I could show off my good qualities." If you feel upset or regret the action, the transgression is incomplete.

Having no shame or consideration for others

You do not care about the consequences of the action for yourself or for others. You are careless in karma; you do not feel that the action has anything to do with your karma.

The eighteen root vows

You must abandon the following.

1. Praising yourself or belittling others out of an attachment to receiving offerings or admiration.
2. Even though you are able, not giving material aid to others through miserliness; or not teaching Dharma to those who are suffering and without a protector because you want to amass knowledge for yourself alone.
3. Not forgiving others but harbouring a grudge and continuing to do so even when they apologize.
4. Abandoning the Mahayana teachings by saying that some of its tenets (*pitaka*, literally "baskets") are not teachings of the Buddha and propounding your own fabricated or perverted doctrine.
5. Taking back offerings to the Buddha, Dharma and Sangha or taking them by robbery or devious schemes; using for your own purpose material dedicated to the Sangha.
6. Abandoning or despising the holy Dharma by denigrating the scriptures or practices of any of the three vehicles of the *sravakas*, the Pratyekabuddhas, or the bodhisattvas; if you have an inclination for tantra, criticizing the Paramitayana; if you are inclined towards the Mahayana, criticizing the Hinayana and vice versa. You should not criticize the differences between various teachings, because Buddha taught with skilful means, in various ways, to guide disciples with different dispositions. This criticism is more serious than destroying all the stupas on earth.

7. Harming an ordained person, inflicting violence on them, stealing their robes, or causing them to lose their vows.

8. Committing any of the five heinous actions (to kill your mother, your father, or an *arhat*; to cause disunity among the sangha; to wound a Buddha).

9. Cultivating and holding wrong views such as sectarianism, denying the existence of the Three Jewels, or denying the existence of the law of cause and effect.

10. Destroying any town or country, such as by fire, bombs, pollution, black magic, and so forth.

11. Teaching the doctrine of emptiness to those who are untrained or not ready to understand it. This could be harmful by engendering fear and causing the other person to abandon bodhicitta, thus falling to the level of Hinayana.

12. Turning someone away from working to attain enlightenment and encouraging him to work merely for his own liberation: for example, if someone is training in bodhicitta, saying to that person, "If you practise this, you will never attain enlightenment. Would it not be better to train in Hinayana? At least you will be free from samsara."

13. Encouraging others to abandon their *Pratimoksha* vows: for example, if someone is abiding by his vows, saying, "What is the use of that? Would it not be better to train in bodhicitta, whereby your non-virtues of body, speech and mind will automatically subside?" If that person abandons his or her *Pratimoksha* vows, you have created a transgression. Saying that the *Pratimoksha* vows are not necessary for Mahayana practice is wrong. They are the best exercise.

14. Causing others to share the incorrect views that you might hold regarding the Hinayana teachings, such as saying that, by practising the Hinayana, one can never give up attachment or be released from suffering and delusions. If the other person believes you, it is a transgression.

15. Proclaiming falsely to have realized emptiness. Although you have not understood the doctrine, teaching others, "If you meditate on this, you will be like me and you will understand emptiness directly." This cheats others though pretence. If the other person believes you have realized emptiness, it is a transgression.

16. Accepting as a gift anything you know to have been stolen or embezzled from the Three Jewels or from a bhikshu.

17. Taking material from someone who is meditating on calm abiding and giving it to someone who merely recites texts. Such an action may cause the meditator to abandon his or her practice.

18. Abandoning bodhicitta by thinking "I cannot help sentient beings" or "I do not want to help this particular sentient being".

The forty-six branch vows

You must abandon the following.

(Vows 1-7 concern the perfection of generosity)

1. Not making offerings every day to the Three Jewels with your body, speech and mind, by making prostrations, offering praises and meditating on their qualities.

2. Without trying to oppose your greed or dissatisfaction with what you have, following the mind that strives to accumulate more.

3. Not showing respect for those who are older or have taken these vows before you. You should not think that you are equal or compete with them. It is better to make offerings to them. To respect masters increases your knowledge and brings prosperity to the place.

4. Through hatred or laziness, not answering, or giving wrong or distorted answers to, sincerely asked questions that you are capable of answering.

5. Not accepting invitations or offering of food or clothes from others because of either anger – wanting to hurt the other person's feelings; pride – considering yourself of too high a rank to be seen with humble people; or jealousy – thinking that others of a higher rank than yourself will look upon you with scorn if you are with humble people.

6. Not accepting gifts of money, gold and so forth from others, such as a sponsor, because of anger, pride, jealousy, laziness or harbouring a grudge. Not accepting out of compassion, seeing that the person will be short of that item, is not a transgression of this vow.

7. Out of hatred, laziness, jealousy, miserliness, a grudge or negligence, not giving teachings to someone who is interested and sincerely approaches you for Dharma. You should not think of your own hardship in giving teachings.

(Vows 8–16 concern the perfection of morality)

8. Ignoring, belittling, not forgiving and not helping those who have broken their moral discipline by cultivating the ten immoralities, defiling their *Pratimoksha* vows, committing the five uninterrupted crimes or breaking a root bodhisattva vow. Instead of being hateful and disdainful, you should generate compassion.

9. Not instilling faith in those who follow a path that is not your own practice or your main interest. For example, if a follower of the Hinayana desires that kind of teaching, it should be given so that he develops faith in that path. If you refuse to give a requested teaching that you are qualified to teach, it is a transgression.

10. Not committing one of the seven non-virtuous actions of the body and speech with a bodhicitta motivation if circumstances deem it necessary, by saying that to do so goes against *vinaya*. By preoccupying yourself with small activities, you may miss an opportunity to help sentient beings. For example, in the *vinaya* it is stated that saffron robes must be blessed. This is important for the Hinayana, but one who is on the bodhisattva path may use his time for greater purposes. If you have an opportunity to benefit others without committing a fault, you transgress this vow by rigidly adhering to the *vinaya* and the seven virtues of body and speech, thus hindering your opportunity to help.

11. Not committing one of the seven non-virtues of body and speech to benefit others out of compassion. If circumstances deem it necessary, a bodhisattva is allowed to commit one of these non-virtues and must do so. However, you must be very careful. Without having realized bodhicitta, it is difficult to transform into virtue the seven non-virtues of body and speech.

12. Accepting material that has been gained by yourself or others through one of the five wrong livelihoods:

    (a) flattery: praising others to gain something for yourself

    (b) hinting: such as saying, "The gift that you gave before was so nice", thereby implying that you want more

    (c) bribery: giving a small thing to receive a larger one

    (d) extortion or blackmail: putting pressure on somebody so that he has no choice

    (e) hypocrisy: changing your usual actions to make a good impression so that others will give you something.

13. Having your main interest in idle gossip and frivolous activities, such as dancing, playing sports, listening to the radio, drinking, or involv-

ing others in frivolous talk. All of these cause your mind to wander, and you waste time that could be used to practise Dharma.

14. Wrongly thinking that, because bodhisattvas remain in samsara for three countless great aeons and are not afraid of delusions, it is not necessary to try to abandon delusions and achieve Nirvana. This is faulty thinking. Bodhisattvas come to this world to benefit sentient beings, but they have an even greater renunciation of samsara and wish for Nirvana than Hinayana practitioners. But in their great compassion they will happily be reborn in the *naraks* if this will benefit just one sentient being. So it is mistaken not to cultivate the opponents to the delusions and to try to achieve Nirvana or dissuade others from trying to attain enlightenment because of the above wrong view.

15. Not trying to avoid a bad reputation or not abandoning the poor habits of body and speech that are the cause of your bad reputation. In order to be more effective at helping others, you need to abandon notoriety. You must try to dispel a bad reputation, whether it is deserved or not, so that you can benefit others. Any other motivation is part of the eight worldly Dharmas.

16. Not correcting the deluded actions of others when you are capable of doing so – that is, not pointing out somebody's negative habits of body or speech. When wrathfulness would be beneficial, not punishing a non-virtuous person to correct him because you think it would hurt his feelings or because you fear his anger.

(Vows 17–20 concern the perfection of patience)

17. Becoming angry and retaliating with your body, speech or mind when you are insulted, blamed, beaten or the object of somebody's anger, or when your shortcomings are exposed to others.

18. Rejecting someone who is angry with you. Through harmful intent, anger or just laziness, ignoring the angry person and not trying to alleviate the situation that made him angry by explaining why you acted as you did, pacifying him or apologizing to him.

19. Refusing to accept the sincere apologies of others out of anger or laziness. This differs from the root vow because the four conditions are not needed to transgress it.

20. Following your anger and not trying to abandon it; feeding your anger by thinking that you acted rightly. Instead, you should contemplate the disadvantages of anger.

(Vows 21–3 concern the perfection of perseverance)

21. Giving teachings, having disciples, building monasteries or gathering people for the purpose of receiving reputation, profit or remuneration. You should have Dharma gatherings with the intention to benefit others and make them receive enlightenment.

22. Not eliminating laziness, procrastination, delusions of incapability, and sleep, which are detrimental to your practice, and wasting time and energy on the trivial matters of samsara. You should avoid sleeping late or irregularly.

23. Passing time by frivolously talking about objects of attachment.

(Vows 24–6 concern samadhi, the perfection of concentration)

24. Not making an effort to study the means of attaining samadhi through requesting the guru for teachings. If you desire to meditate, you must approach your guru for instruction. The transgression is not to do this because of laziness, evil intent, arrogance or meditating on samadhi without teachings.

25. Not trying to eliminate the obstacles that hinder your attaining samadhi. The five obstacles in particular are: attachment to the desire realm and the five sense objects; harmful intent; sleep and woolly-mindedness; regret and agitation; doubt.

26. Attachment to the bliss of remaining in samadhi without doing any other virtuous activities, or deliberately concentrating for the sake of this bliss. Thinking that samadhi is a special kind of knowledge, and thus not having the strong wish to progress further.

(Vows 27–34 concern the perfection of wisdom)

27. Looking down on Hinayana scriptures and saying the study of them is not necessary for Mahayanists.

28. Learning Hinayana discourses and practices if you have the time and ability to learn the Mahayana and are already engaged in those of the Mahayana.

29. Making an unnecessary study of non-Buddhist scriptures, thus neglecting to study the Buddha's teachings. Although such study is permitted and is advantageous for understanding and helping others, you should not use excessive time and energy in studying non-Buddhist tenets.

30. Favouring, becoming attached to, or cultivating interest in non-Buddhist teachings when you have to study them. You are allowed to study non-Buddhist texts so that you can refute wrong views; but you transgress if, instead of doing this, you become fond of these scriptures.

31. Casting aspersions on the Mahayana teachings, the guru or the subject, such as saying a scripture is poor in subject matter, composition or power to help sentient beings, or that the subject is boring.
32. Praising yourself or belittling others out of anger or arrogance.
33. Not attending discourses, debates, discussions, *pujas* or ceremonies because of arrogance, laziness or anger.
34. Not respecting but abusing the guru who gives teachings and shows the path, seeking only his words without contemplation of their meaning.

(Vows 35–46 concern the perfection of the morality of helping others)
35. Not helping those in need of help when you have the capacity to do so. Eight ways of helping sentient beings are specified.
    (1) Not helping those doing purposeful work who ask for help, by making excuses or by being lazy.
    (2) Not helping those who are on a journey, who need help carrying things or need protection, because of laziness.
    (3) Not teaching language and Dharma to those who ask.
    (4) Not doing work which may not be Dharma, but which concerns Dharma, for those who ask.
    (5) Not helping someone who asks you to protect their possessions if you have the time and ability.
    (6) Not helping to unify a couple who ask for your help.
    (7) Not eating a meal, if you have the time and ability, with those who ask.
    (8) Not going, if invited, to create merits, such as to a *puja*, if you have the time and ability.
36. Not helping sick persons with materials or service because of hatred or laziness.
37. Not working to alleviate suffering but instead avoiding to help eliminate it through anger, laziness, or negligence. This refers to people such as the blind, deaf, paralysed, those with missing limbs, those with difficulty in breathing, travellers on a difficult journey, people having the five obstacles (see number 25), those in mental distress, those who are paranoid and those who have lost their authority or position or have been abused by others.
38. Through anger or laziness not exhorting, correcting or activating a lazy person or a person who does not know virtuous from non-virtuous actions. If you see a person engaging in frivolous activities, you

should give timely advice in appropriate situations and under proper circumstances so that people can avoid those actions and engage in virtue.

39. Through anger or laziness not repaying the kindness of someone who has helped you materially or morally.

40. Through harmful intent or laziness not consoling those who are grieving because of separation from their dear ones or possessions.

41. Through harmful intent or laziness not giving food, clothes or other necessities to the poor and needy if you are asked and if you have enough to spare.

42. Through hatred or laziness not working for the welfare of your disciples and attendants, or not giving teachings and/or materials.

43. Being self-assertive and not acting in accordance with the wishes or feelings of others. Through lack of consideration, you do not act according to the level of their mind when you are capable of doing so. The actions that practitioners can do differ according to their level of mind. If you have realized bodhicitta, it is difficult not to transform negative actions of body and speech into virtue. But if your mind is not capable, you cannot do these actions even if others request you to do them. However, you can act in small ways to help others according to the level of their minds. By being well mannered, you please them and encourage them in the Dharma. Transgressions of this vow occur if you are with a Dharma practitioner and you lie down in comfort without being concerned about others. Or you may be with worldly people and use bad manners, which cause them to become angry or lose their devotion.

44. Not praising those deserving praise, or not rejoicing in others who praise learned and realized beings.

45. Not preventing those doing harmful actions from continuing their actions by whatever means is necessary according to the circumstances. The boastful may need to be looked down upon; the violent punished physically; those harmful to society banished. Out of laziness or attachments to those people, you do not act when you have the authority to do so. Abbots and disciplinarians should punish or reprimand those who are misbehaving. Transgression consists in having the power to do something and not doing it because you do not care about the harmful person himself or about those he is harming, or because you are lazy.

46. If you possess psychic powers, not using them in a time of need, such as to frighten someone who is about to do a non-virtuous action so that he will stop, to enhance others' faith, or to subdue them.

This translation, with explanatory commentary, was dictated by Lama Zopa Rinpoche in the early 1970s and first published in 1974. It is reprinted here, with minor emendations, from the third revised edition by Ven. Constance Miller, FPMT Education Services (FPMT Education Department, 2000).

Notes

NOTES TO THE INTRODUCTION (PAGES 1–44)

1. Some scholars, however, have suggested that *sattva* in *bodhisattva* is a false sanskritization of an original Prakrit word meaning "directed towards" or "focused on".
2. Charles D. Orzech, "Mahavairocana", *The Encyclopedia of Religion*, ed. Mircea Eliade, p. 126.
3. "Buddhist Ethics", ibid., p. 500.
4. Ibid., p. 501.
5. Paul Groner, in *Chinese Buddhist Apocrypha*, ed. Robert E. Buswell Jr.
6. Similar to these are the injunctions against praising oneself and belittling others (first root vow and thirty-second branch vow) and against miserliness (second root vow). In the same way, one is asked not to harm an ordained person (seventh root vow) and not to destroy any town or country (tenth root vow). One is also encouraged to show respect for the elders (third branch vow) and not to give distorted answers to questions on the Dharma (fourth branch vow). As in the *Brahma's Net Sutra*, one is admonished for not giving teaching to someone who is interested (seventh branch vow). Moreover, one is asked not to become angry (seventeenth branch vow) and not to harbour anger (twentieth branch vow). There are also concerns about refusing to accept sincere apologies (nineteenth branch vow), making unnecessary study of non-Buddhist teachings (twenty-ninth), casting aspersions on the Mahayana teachings (thirty-first), not paying attention to discourses (thirty-third), not helping sick persons (thirty-sixth), not working to alleviate suffering (thirty-seventh),

and not giving food to the poor and needy (forty-first branch vow).

7. Kenneth Ch'en , *Buddhism in China*, pp. 367, 368.

8. *The Long Discourses of the Buddha*, tr. Maurice Walshe, pp. 466–7.

9. Kenneth Ch'en, *The Chinese Transformation of Buddhism*, p. 19.

10. This Chinese text is not to be confused with the Pali *Brahma's Net Sutta* (*Brahmajala Sutta*; *Digha Nikaya* 1), which is a study of wrong views.

11. *The Long Discourses of the Buddha*, tr. Maurice Walshe, pp. 133–41.

NOTES TO THE BODHISATTVA PRECEPTS (PAGES 45–93)

1. Devoted: the Chinese literally means "filial piety" or being "filial and obedient", but I felt that devoted, devout, devotion would work better throughout the text. It is this term that makes the present text an essentially original Chinese Buddhist scripture (see Introduction). For that reason its subsequent occurrences will be noted as 1a, 1b etc.

   1a. Idem.

   1b. Idem.

   1c. Idem.

   1d. Idem.

   1e. Idem.

   1f. Idem.

   1g. Idem.

   1h. Idem.

   1i. Idem.

   1j. Idem.

   1k. Idem.

   1l. Idem; here note that the parents are mentioned before the teacher in terms of devotion.

   1m. Idem.

   1n. Idem; cf. 1l.

   1o. Idem.

2. This last sentence is not found in the text that I used, either in the Chinese or in the Korean vernacular translation, but it was in other versions of the Chinese text that I consulted.

3. This is another theme that recurs in these precepts: self-relinquishing. Though quite extreme and perhaps shocking to modern sensibility, it

seems to have been a common metaphor in China at that time for expressing utter devotion and generosity. Subsequent appearances are noted as 3a, 3b etc.

3a. Idem.

3b. Idem.

3c. Idem. This, the most extreme instance of this kind of metaphorical declaration, might seem to contradict the injunction not to hurt oneself. It had however already appeared in the legendary lives of Shakyamuni Buddha, who to cultivate generosity, compassion and self-abnegation even gave his body to be eaten by a hungry tigress. His example is meant to inspire great aspiration and determination.

3d. Idem.

3e. Idem.

4. In Korea to this day all temples belonging to the celibate order of Buddhist monks and nuns are vegetarian, as is the case in China, Taiwan and Hongkong.

5. In Korean and Chinese temples, all these pungent vegetables are avoided to this day. The prohibition seems to come from the yogic tradition in India, which considered such vegetables to be disturbing to the temperament and to provoke heat and possibly lust.

6. This sentence is found in the printed Chinese text included with the Korean translation but not translated into Korean. Some scholars think the reference could be to a larger text from which the *Brahma's Net Sutra* was extracted, though no such text was ever found. The reference may have been added to give more authenticity to the text.

6a. Idem.

6b. Idem.

6c. Idem.

6d. Idem.

6e. Idem.

7. This term refers to monastics – men or women – who have left home and shaved their heads, and who now live a celibate life in a monastery or nunnery.

8. In the Korean translation, the title of this precept refers only to the "proper times"; in some Chinese versions only the second part, about "not interfering with laypeople", is given. I chose to put the two together to be representative of both the Korean and the Chinese.

9. Of course, the major precepts prohibit killing. Here the point is emphasized that killing is not permitted; and that it would be doubly

bad to influence someone to do it on a day where one is supposed to be fasting and pure.

10. The reference is to a story from the time of the Buddha. A monk was set upon by bandits, who took all his belongings and left him naked. They tied his hands to long grass growing in the ground, knowing that he would not free himself and run after them because to uproot the grass would kill it. And he waited for passers-by to release him by unknotting the grass.

11. This is according to the lunar calendar.

12. My teacher, Master Kusan, used to say a few words *sotto voce* whenever he encountered an animal; if at all possible he would also pat it on the head while reciting a mantra.

Glossary

Abhidharma

Literally "special doctrine". The third section of the Buddhist Canon, dedicated to psychological and philosophical treatises.

Acarya

A spiritual teacher, a Dharma master. One of correct conduct who is able to teach others.

Adamantine Buddha

Vajra-Buddha. Vairocana, the sun-Buddha. Sometimes applied to Shakyamuni as embodiment of the truth, wisdom and purity.

Amitabha Buddha

The Buddha responsible for the creation of the western Pure Land through the force of his forty-eight vows to save sentient beings.

Arhat

One who has attained Nirvana through freeing himself or herself from the origins of suffering, delusion and craving.

Avatamsaka Sutra

The "Flower Adornment" scripture is a seminal text about the stages of the bodhisattva path and the interpenetration of all things. It was very influential in Chinese Buddhism. The first Chinese translation appeared in 420.

Avici

In Buddhist cosmology, the deepest of the eight hot hells, where beings are subjected to uninterrupted torments.

Awakening

The realization of the Buddha, available to all.

Bhikshu

A religious mendicant; one who has left home, been fully ordained and depends on alms for a living; a fully ordained Buddhist monk.

Bhikshuni

A fully ordained Buddhist nun, the female counterpart of a bhikshu. The first woman to be ordained was the Buddha's aunt Mahaprajapati, who had nursed him. In the fourteenth year after his enlightenment the Buddha yielded to persuasion and admitted his aunt and women to his order of religious mendicants.

Bodhi

"Awakening". The supreme wisdom of a Buddha.

Bodhicitta (Bodhichitta)

Literally "awakening mind". The aspiration to attain Buddhahood for the sake of all living beings.

Bodhimandala

The place where a Buddha attains the truth of Nirvana, especially that where Shakyamuni attained it.

Bodhisattva

Literally "awakening being". One who aspires to become a Buddha. The notion of the bodhisattva is one of the characteristic features of the Mahayana. The earliest interpretation embraced all beings with a mind for the truth; later it came to denote a conscious being aspiring to awakening for the sake of all. It is also interpreted in terms of leadership and heroism. In general a bodhisattva is a Mahayanist seeking Buddhahood, but from altruistic motives: whether monk or nun, layman or laywoman, one seeks awakening in order to awaken others, and one will sacrifice oneself to save others; one is selfless and devoted to helping others. All conscious beings having the Buddha-nature are natural bodhisattvas who need to practise the way. The mahasattva is sufficiently advanced to become a Buddha, but in accordance with his vow he defers complete Nirvana to save all other conscious beings.

Bodhi tree

"Awakening tree": *Ficus religiosa* (pipal tree). The tree under which Shakyamuni attained enlightenment and became Buddha, situated in Bodh-Gaya, a village in Central North India. To this day its leaves are kept as relics. Cuttings from the original tree were taken to Sri Lanka, and cuttings from the tree that grew from them were taken back in turn after the tree in India was destroyed.

Brahma

In Buddhism, a worldly deity inhabiting the realm of form.

Buddha

"Awakened one".

Buddha Maitreya

The forthcoming Buddha, now in the Tusita Heaven. Considered greatly loving, he presides over the spread of the teaching and protects it. He is regarded as the next enlightened world teacher expected to appear on earth.

Buddha Shakyamuni

The historical Buddha Gautama, born about two and a half thousand years ago in India.

Causal conditions

Reference to the Buddhist principle of "cause and effect": "every cause has an effect, as every effect arises out of a cause". In the present context, primary causes rather than environmental or secondary causes.

Celestial beings

Divine beings, deities.

Chakravatin

Literally "wheel ruler". An emperor or a sovereign of the world, the wheels of whose chariot roll everywhere without obstruction.

Dharma

"Law". A Sanskrit term meaning either the teaching of Buddhism; principle or law; or phenomena in general.

Dharma-body (*dharmakaya*)

The truth body of the Buddha; the spiritual principle of Buddhahood.

Diamond treasure precepts

The Mahayana rules according to the *Brahma's Net Sutra*.

Eight difficult conditions

The eight conditions in which it is difficult to see a Buddha or hear his Dharma: in the hells, as hungry ghosts, as animals, in the Northern continent where all is pleasant (Uttarakura), in the long-life heavens (where life is long and easy), as deaf, blind and dumb, as a worldly philosopher, in the intermediate period between a Buddha and his successor.

Eighteen articles a monk should carry

Willow twigs, soap, the three garments, a water bottle, a begging bowl, mat, staff, censer, filter, handkerchief, knife, fire-producer, pincers, hammock, sutra, the *vinaya*, a Buddha's image and bodhisattva image(s).

Eighteen realms of Brahma

The eighteen heavens of form.

Eight fields of blessings

There are different lists. Here the reference is to the first one.
(1) Buddhas, *arhats*, spiritual teachers, spiritual masters, community of monks, father, mother, the sick.
(2) To make roads and wells; construct canals and bridges; repair dangerous roads; be dutiful to parents; support monks; tend

the sick; save from disaster or distress; provide for a quin-
quennial assembly.
(3) Serving the three precious ones, parents, monks as teachers, the
poor, the sick, animals.

Eight kinds of demon

Demi-gods (*gandharvas*), demons (*pisacas*), demons of monstrous
forms (*kumbhandas*), hungry ghosts (*pretas*), water demons
(*nagas*), female demons (*putanas*), wild demons (*yaksas*) and evil
spirits (*raksasas*).

Five hundred *arhats*

Five hundred great *arhats* who formed the synod under Kaniska
and are the supposed compilers of the *Abhidharma-mahavib-
hasa-sastra*, 400 years after Buddha entered Nirvana. The 500
*arhat*s (*lohans*) found in Chinese monasteries have various definitions.

Forty bodhisattva stages

They are classified in four groups in the *Brahma's Net Sutra*:
(1) Ten Initial Stages: renunciation, ethics, patience, zeal, meditation, wisdom, resolve, guarding the Dharma, joy, blessing (by
the Buddha). These are associated with the ten dwellings.
(2) Ten Developmental Stages: loving-kindness, compassion, joy,
renunciation, almsgiving, good discourse, altruism, mutuality,
meditation, wisdom. These are associated with the ten con-
ducts.
(3) Ten Diamond Stages: faith, remembrance, transference of one's
merits to others, understanding, uprightness, no-retreat,
Mahayana, formlessness, wisdom, indestructibility. These are
associated with the ten transferences.
(4) Ten Grounds (see below).

Fourfold assembly

Bhikshus, bhikshunis, laymen and laywomen.

Go

An oriental game with black and white pieces, not unlike draughts.

Heretical views

Views of outsiders, of other cults, of non-Buddhist doctrines. There are many groups of these: Vishnuites, Shivaites, Sankhya philosophy, etc.

Hinayana

"Small vehicle". This term refers to the traditions that developed immediately after Shakyamuni Buddha's death until the first century CE when Mahayana doctrines were introduced.

Itinerant ascetic practices (*dhuta*)

There are twelve itinerant ascetic practices relating to release from ties to clothing, food and dwelling: wearing garments of cast-off rags; wearing only the three garments; eating only food that has been begged; eating only breakfast and the midday meal; eating no food between the two; eating a limited amount; dwelling as a hermit; living among tombs; living under a tree; living under the open sky; having no fixed dwelling place; sitting and not lying down.

Jambudvipa

In every universe in ancient Buddhist cosmology there are four inhabited continents, of which Jambudvipa is one. It is situated south of Mt Meru, considered the centre of the world as known to the early Indians. This view was incorporated by the Buddhists in their vision of the universe.

Kapilavastu

Capital of Shakya, situated about 100 miles due north of Benares, north-west of present Gorakhpur.

Kasaya

Originally ochre, the colour of the monk's robes in India, it now refers to the monk's or nun's robes themselves. The word is interpreted as meaning dyed, so as to distinguish it from the normal colour of the dress of the people of the country.

Li

A Chinese measure of distance, about 500 metres.

Lord Indra

Lord of the gods of the sky. In Buddhism he represents secular power and is inferior to a Buddhist saint.

Lotus Platform Treasury

The lotus world or universe of each Buddha for his "body of delight" (*sambhogakaya*). Also a lotus throne for images of Buddhas and bodhisattvas.

Mahasthavira

Old man, elder, head monk, abbot. A monk of between twenty and forty-nine years' standing.

Mahasattva

Literally "great being", a title given to Buddhas, bodhisattvas, and other enlightened beings.

Mahayana

"Great Vehicle". A name for the teachings of the Buddha that deal with the bodhisattva's path to enlightenment. It is the greater vehicle in comparison with the small vehicle (Hinayana). Mahayana is the form of Buddhism prevalent in Tibet, Mongolia, China, Korea, Japan and in other places in the Far East.

Mahesvara

The celestial king of the sixth desire-heaven.

Mantra

An incantation; a mystical formula usually composed of Sanskrit syllables. Often associated with a particular Buddha or bodhisattva, it is recited in a continuous and repetitive manner.

Mind-Ground

Mind from which all springs; the mental ground or conditions. The third of the three agents: body, mouth, mind.

Nature

The Buddha-nature immanent in all beings.

Nirvana

The quiescent state realized though the cessation of suffering, delusion and craving. It also refers to the passing away of the Buddha as in "after the Nirvana of the Buddha".

Pali

The ancient mid-Indic language in which one of the earliest canons of the Buddha Shakyamuni's discourses is recorded.

Perfections (*paramitas*)

Perfections that must be cultivated in Mahayana Buddhism. They fall into two groups, one of six and one of ten. The six perfections are: generosity, morality, patience, effort, meditation and wisdom. The ten perfections are these six plus adaptability (teaching as suited to the occasion and hearer), vows, force of purpose and knowledge.

Pratimoksha

Code of discipline: in general, it refers to the rules for monks and nuns found in the *vinaya* texts. They should be read in assembly twice a month, at which time each monk or nun is invited to confess any violations.

Pratyekabuddha

"Silent Buddha". As seen by the Mahayana, one who seeks enlightenment for oneself without depending on a teacher. Someone who has achieved great realization but does not teach or save others.

Puja

A religious ceremony.

Rocana Buddha

"Belonging to or coming from the sun". According to the *Avatam-saka Sutra*, the Buddha whose body is said symbolically to constitute the universe; he can also represent the enjoyment body of the Buddha.

Samadhi

A meditative state of concentration.

Samanthabadra Bodhisattva

"The universally good", one of the four great bodhisattvas in Mahayana Chinese Buddhism. He is usually seated on a white elephant, and is often regarded as the personification of great action.

Samsara

The cycle of birth and death.

Sangha

"Community". The community of people committed to the practice of Dharma, sometimes used exclusively to refer to ordained monks and nuns.

Seven Buddhas

The seven ancient Buddhas: Vipasyin, Sikhin, Visvabhu, Krakucchanda, Kanakamuni, Kasyapa and Shakyamuni.

Seven heinous crimes

Shedding the blood of a Buddha, killing one's father, mother, a spiritual teacher or a spiritual master, subverting or disrupting the monastic community and killing an *arhat*. This list is specific to the *Brahma's Net Sutra*. Generally the list is of five heinous crimes: killing one's mother, father or an *arhat*, causing disunity in the sangha and wounding a Buddha.

Seven kinds of jewel

There are various descriptions. A common one is: gold, silver, lapis lazuli, crystal, agate, rubies or red pearls, cornelian.

Sila

"Precept", "discipline". It refers to the various sets of Buddhist precepts.

Six kinds of close relative

The six closest relations: father, mother, wife and child, elder and younger siblings.

Six realms

The six regions of existence in Buddhist cosmology: the abodes of the celestials, titans, humans, animals, hungry ghosts and denizens of hells.

Six specified fasting days

The six monthly fast days: 8th, 14th, 15th, 23rd, 29th and 30th. These are the days on which the four heavenly kings take note of human conduct and when evil demons are abroad, so that great care is required and nothing should be eaten after midday, hence the fast.

Six times of day and night

The six "hours" or periods in a day (three for night and three for day): morning, noon and evening; night, midnight and dawn. Also the six divisions of the year: two each of spring, summer and winter.

Sixteen countries

The sixteen ancient kingdoms of Buddhist India: Vaisali, Kosala, Sravasti, Magadha, Baranasi, Kapilavastu, Kusinagara, Kausambi, Pancala, Pataliputra, Mathura, Usa, Punyavardhana, Devavatara, Kasi and Campa.

Sravaka

"Hearer", "disciple": either one who has heard (the voice of the Buddha), or the lowest degree of attainment, the others being Pratyekabuddha, bodhisattva, Buddha.

Stupa

A reliquary in which remains of the Buddha and enlightened teachers are preserved, which has become an architectural symbol of enlightenment.

Summer rains retreat

The traditional three-month retreat during the summer rains of South-East Asia (mid July to mid October). It is generally an intense period of meditation and study during which monks and nuns do not move from their place of residence. In Korea there are two three-month retreats, one each in the winter and the summer.

Sutra (Sanskrit), Sutta (Pali)

A "warp": threads woven lengthwise. Laws, canons, classical Buddhist works; a discourse given by a Buddha.

Tathagata

"Thus come or thus gone". One of the traditional epithets given to the Buddha, who often referred to himself by this name.

Ten Developmental Stages

See Forty bodhisattva stages.

Ten Diamond Stages

See Forty bodhisattva stages.

Ten directions

The ten directions of space: the eight points of the compass, the zenith and the nadir.

Ten Grounds

The ten fundamental Grounds or Stages of Mahayana bodhisattva development are generally: joy, purity, luminosity, radiance, difficult to conquer, presence, far-reaching, immovability, good wisdom, Dharma-clouds.

The ten Grounds as found in the *Brahma's Net Sutra* are: equality, fine wisdom, light, brilliant flame, illuminating wisdom, beautiful brightness, accomplishment, Buddha's roar, flower adornment, entrance into the Buddha's realm.

Ten Initial Stages

See Forty bodhisattva stages.

Ten major transgressions

Breaking the ten major precepts: killing, stealing, improper sexual behaviour, lying, selling alcohol, discussing the faults of others, praising oneself while slandering others, reviling others in order to spare oneself, being angry and not forgiving, slandering the Three Jewels.

Ten modes of meditation

Ten modes of contemplating the universe from ten aspects: from the viewpoint of earth, water, fire, wind, blue, yellow, red, white, space or mind. For example, contemplated under the aspect of water, then the universe is regarded as in flux and change.

Ten vows

See Vows (Ten).

Thousand Buddhas

Each aeon – past, present, future – has a thousand Buddhas.

Three Jewels

Buddha, Dharma and Sangha.

Three periods

Past, present and future. The universe is described as eternally in motion, like a flowing stream. The Buddhas of the past, present and future are Kasyapa, Shakyamuni and Maitreya.

Three special months of abstinence and care

The first, fifth and ninth lunar months.

Three thousand worlds

A way of describing the universe.

Three unfortunate realms

The three difficult realms in which to be reincarnated: hells, hungry ghosts and animals.

Twelve categories of sutra

Twelve divisions of the Mahayana canon: *sutra, geya, gatha, nidana, jataka, abhidharma, avadana, upadesa, udana, vaipulya, vyakarana* and *vinaya*.

Upadhyaya

Lecturer, *vinaya* preceptor, teacher of Buddhism. The teacher who is responsible for the observance of the various ceremonies, regulations and precepts.

Uposatha

A fast day. Also the bi-monthly ceremony during which the *Pratimoksha* is recited, after the monks or nuns have heard each other's confession.

Vinaya

Ethical discipline. The body of ethical rules and disciplines for Buddhist monks and nuns and for laypeople, prescribed by the Buddha.

Vow

The vow of perfection, the eighth of the ten *paramitas*. The bodhi-sattva's vow to attain awakening and help all beings to cross to the shore of awakening.

Vows (Ten)

As found in the *Brahma's Net Sutra*:
    To be faithful and devoted to parents, teachers and sangha
    To find good teachers
    To meet virtuous friends
    To learn from teachers and virtuous friends
    To understand the ten Initial Stages
    To understand the ten Developmental Stages
    To understand the ten Diamond Stages
    To understand the ten Grounds
    To practise in accordance with the Dharma
    To maintain the Bodhisattva precepts.

Bibliography

Bechert, Heinz, and Richard Gombrich (eds), *The World of Buddhism* (London: Thames and Hudson, 1984)

Buswell, Robert E., Jr (ed.), *Chinese Buddhist Apocrypha* (Hawaii: University of Hawaii Press, 1990)

—— (tr.), *The Collected Works of Chinul* (Hawaii: University of Hawaii Press, 1983)

Ch'en, Kenneth, *Buddhism in China* (Princeton: Princeton University Press, 1964)

——, *The Chinese Transformation of Buddhism* (Princeton: Princeton University Press, 1973)

De Groot, J. J. M., *Le Code du Mahayana en Chine* (Amsterdam: Verhider Kon. Ak. Van Wetensch, 1893)

Dharma Realm Buddhist University (tr.), with commentary by Master Hui Seng, *The Buddha Speaks the Brahma Net Sutra*, 2 vols (Talmage, CA: Buddhist Text Translation Society, 1981)

Eliade, Mircea (ed.), *The Encyclopedia of Religion* (New York and London: Macmillan, 1987, 1996)

Elisseeff, Serge, "The Bonmokyo and the Great Buddha of Todai-ji", *Harvard Journal of Asiatic Studies* (1936), **1**:84–96

Hobogirin (Dictionnaire encyclopédique du Bouddhisme) (Paris: Institut de France, 1929–)

Kuo Li Ying, *Confession et contrition dans le Bouddhisme chinois du Ve au Xe siècle* (Paris: École française de l'Extrême-Orient, 1994)

Nearman, Rev. Hubert (tr.), "Scripture of Brahma's Net", in *Buddhist Writings* (Mount Shasta, CA: Shasta Abbey Press, 1994)

Shantideva, tr. Stephen Batchelor, *A Guide to the Bodhisattva's Way of Life* (Dharamsala: Library of Tibetan Works and Archives, 1979)

Soto Shu Sutras (Tokyo: Soto Shu Shumucho, 1982)

Walshe, Maurice (tr.), *The Long Discourses of the Buddha* (*Digha Nikaya*) (Boston, MA: Wisdom Publications, 1987)

Zurcher, E., *The Buddhist Conquest of China*, Sinica Leidensia (Leiden, 1959)